Praise f
Coach Yourself Confident

I devoured every page of this wonderfully written book. Whether you have been in front of the mirror for a long time or you are at the start of your journey, you will find a remarkable guide to navigate the land of your own confidence. Having personally gone through many comings and goings, I can attest that this is a worthwhile investment. As Julie intelligently puts it: 'While confidence does not guarantee success, it does stack the odds in your favour.'

Sergio Ezama, Chief Talent Officer, Netflix

Utterly brilliant. This is a book that is easy to read, incisive and thought provoking. The exercises do a great job of encouraging you to slow down, reflect and apply. As someone that has spent much of my career dealing with confidence peaks and troughs, Julie's book is the perfect tonic! A must read for so many of us!

Francesca Theokli, Marketing Director and Executive Leadership Team, Weetabix Food Company

This book is written in such an accessible voice. As I read Julie's words, I felt like I was in the room with my own personal coach. The activities made me really stop, think and reflect. The references to external experts and 'real-life' experiences frequently prompted a smile of recognition.

Being a high performer means also being kind to yourself. This book leads you through that journey. If only my less experienced self could have read this all those years ago.
Rachel King, Group People Director, Spire Healthcare

I'm quoted in the book, so I'm probably supposed to have it all together in terms of confidence. But confidence is not a box to be ticked. It's more like a muscle: if you stop working it, it shrinks. I've been exploring new opportunities since retiring from professional sport, and while it has been fun, it's hard to move from an environment in which you are one of the best to environments where you are a beginner. I know it takes time to learn and gain experience, but I certainly don't want to prolong that with a self-imposed 'self-doubt tax'. I really appreciate the way Julie has opened my eyes to habits and behaviours that are getting in my way. I suspect this is a book I will come back to regularly for a confidence workout!
Stef Reid MBE, Paralympian, Keynote Speaker and Broadcaster

I loved *Coach Yourself Confident* and found myself making a mental note as I read of the people who I want to send copies to. It's readable, accessible and encouraging, and the content really resonated – there were numerous 'aha' moments for me.
Jane Burkitt, Vice President EMEA Supply Chain Operations, The LEGO Group

In *Coach Yourself Confident*, Julie Smith draws from the deep well of her corporate coaching experience to share powerful and practical ways for us to build our own confidence. Her experience, insight and humanity permeates every page, and offers encouragement and practical ways for people who are looking to build inner belief and resilience. A great read, packed full of warmth and wisdom.

Becky Hall, Coach and Author of The Art of Enough

I love this book! It's a very practical guide, crammed full of real client stories, personal experiences and practical exercises. Probably the closest you can get to being coached without the coach – it feels as though Julie is right by your side every step of the way. I'm already recommending it to others!

Emma Smythe, Executive Coach and Director of Leadership Development in Big 4 Consulting firm

Coach Yourself Confident is based on detailed research and contains thoughtful analysis of what confidence is, where it comes from, how to build it and hold onto it. This is combined with practical exercises and advice, which stops you from simply admiring Julie's diagnosis of the issues around confidence and makes you apply her lessons to your own real-life experiences. Highly recommended.

Karen Betts OBE, Chief Executive, Food and Drink Federation

Julie has managed to decode and make practical a way to unlock one of the biggest assets to success – yourself! Taming the inner critic, even training it to be a constructive force is, in my experience, the single biggest shift someone can make as they strive for self-fulfilment. You won't know how tall you are until you get up off your knees. *Coach Yourself Confident* will help you do that!

David Murray, Managing Director UK & Ireland,
pladis Global

Coach Yourself Confident is highly relatable – I found myself smiling in recognition many times. It's pragmatic, providing sensible steps to growing confidence and bringing out your best self. The book gives permission to make mistakes, to be humble and to unlock your potential, rather than trying to be something you are not. It's rich with coaching techniques and stories to bring the topic to life, and Julie's tone is encouraging and supportive.

Lucinda Scott, Customer Service Director, first direct

I was pulled in from page one with the way that Julie appears to tread lightly on some powerful insights, whilst actually guiding you through transformational thinking. The concept of a humble leader, knowing what they are good at, whilst positively reflecting on how they could become even better, really resonated. I learned so much and cannot wait to get it on the reading list of friends and colleagues.

Paul Campbell, Senior Vice President Supply Chain,
PepsiCo Europe

This book was a truly brilliant read and has made a lasting change to my mindset about my own confidence, self-doubt and overall mental well-being. The reframe of confidence as 'trust in self' has been a true unlock for me and the experience of reading this book felt like having a personal coach right by my side supporting and encouraging me to learn and grow.

Michelle Parczuk, Chief People Officer, Avon Cosmetics

JULIE SMITH

coach

yourself

confident

ditch the
self-doubt tax

unlock humble
confidence

First published in Great Britain by Practical Inspiration Publishing, 2024.

Illustrations by Caroline Chapple
© Julie Smith, 2024

The moral rights of the author have been asserted

ISBN   9781788605564 (HB)
        9781788605175 (PB)
        9781788605199 (epub)
        9781788605182 (mobi)

Want to bulk-buy copies of this book for your team and colleagues? We can customize the content and co-brand *Coach Yourself Confident* to suit your business's needs.

Please email info@practicalinspiration.com for more details.

For Dad.

For Jackie.

Two of my biggest believers.

Contents

List of activities

Introduction

How to coach yourself confident

I imagine that you picked up this book because you'd like to be more confident. My experience as a coach has shown me just how widespread this desire is – the desire to grow in confidence. It's striking to me how many of the topics that leaders have brought to coaching conversations over the past 15 years have been underpinned by a need to access a balanced, objective and compassionate self-view. Sometimes the leader arrives at coaching with a stated aim to be more confident. In other cases, it's as we begin to explore the topic at hand that we uncover the impact of a harsh inner critic, an anxiety-inducing fear of failure or a pervasive sense of not being good enough. I've worked with coaching clients whose lack of confidence has masqueraded as a different development need such as strategic thinking, influencing at senior levels, navigating a matrix organization or maintaining home-work balance.

I'd like to be more confident too. Whilst I've managed to drastically diminish the self-doubt that plagued me during the early part of my career, I still allow self-doubt to undermine me at times. My experience has been that as my confidence has grown, so has my ambition. As I gain a feeling of comfort and assurance in one setting, I look to the next opportunity – the next setting in which I'd like to quieten the voice of my self-doubt. Building our confidence is work that is never complete.

I've written this book because I've seen close-up the difference that confidence can make, by its presence and by its absence. I want to share what I have learned through three decades of supporting others to develop, and I believe that in doing so I can support you to grow your confidence.

Mapping out the territory

In the upcoming pages, we'll explore the full territory of confidence, from the insecurity of its absence to the powerful feeling of its presence. Here I'd like to introduce you to some of the key features of the terrain, so that you have an idea of what's to come. First, let's look more closely at what confidence is. 'The word confidence comes from the Latin *confidere*, meaning 'to have full trust'. Confidence is the trust in yourself that whatever the situation, whatever life throws at you, you will be OK. You will have the resources you need, and you will find a way through. Confidence is a quiet, steady feeling of 'I've got this'.

Confidence is not about kidding yourself that you have superpowers, that with a little bit of belief anything is possible. The constraints of reality do still apply. A version of confidence that's about going into a situation thinking 'I can *do* it' attaches significance to the outcome, to the achievement. For me, confidence is more than this. It's a sense of trust in yourself that you will be OK whatever comes *and* whatever the outcome. Your sense of self is defined by neither success nor failure.

Author and activist Glennon Doyle talks about true confidence meaning loyalty to self.[1] Confidence requires self-acceptance: this is me, imperfect and flawed, brilliant and unique. I can be me without fear. I can resist the urge to mould myself into a shape that will please other people. I am enough. Confidence enables you to stand alone, to not be overly attached to what other people think. With confidence comes a robust sense of self, one that is not reliant on the evaluation or reassurance of others. A firm (but not overplayed) sense of trust in your own abilities fuels a willingness to stand out, a willingness to risk the approbation of others, whether by voicing an unpopular opinion or by taking unexpected action.

Confidence propels you forward: it enables you to try new things, to step into new experiences, to stretch, to grow. It's fuel for life. It's an in-the-moment thing (confidence in this situation), and it's an ongoing relationship with yourself (the extent to which you trust yourself to be enough). Confidence can be fickle. It comes and goes, sometimes without any obvious reason. Sometimes the confidence dips are short and

---

[1] Doyle, 2020.

easy to climb back out of. Sometimes something happens to send our self-trust crashing down and it takes time and hard work to put the pieces back together again.

My aim is to support you to grow a particular brand of confidence: humble confidence. In essence, this is an objective and compassionate view of self, underpinned by the humble confidence mantra: I am good enough *and* I can be better. With this form of confidence, our sense of what we are capable of aligns with our skills and abilities. It's a solid and balanced sense of self, with neither inflating egotism nor diminishing self-doubt. And it's a recognition of the truth that there is always room for us to grow and develop. As human beings, we are never the finished article, there is always room to 'be better'. Our striving for better can be fuelled by a thirst for learning and growth, an appetite to improve, not by a compulsion to compensate for something that we lack. There is no lack: we are already good enough.

In our exploration of confidence, we must deepen our understanding of self-doubt, the nagging sense that we don't have what we need to face the situation in which we find ourselves; the questioning of our abilities and our decisions. We all feel self-doubt, with varying degrees of frequency and intensity; it is an unavoidable part of the human experience.

This book does not offer a cure for self-doubt. That would be foolish because self-doubt is not an affliction, it's not something that we need to eradicate. Self-doubt is not inherently a bad thing – when our self-doubt is right-sized, it fuels curiosity, growth and collaboration. Our aim is not to eradicate our self-doubt, but to re-size it. My suggestion is that self-doubt becomes an issue when it is over-sized, when our inner critic – that nagging voice that criticizes, belittles and judges us – is too loud. Over-sized self-doubt can hold us back, and it can lead us to pay the self-doubt tax. This tax is levied in overwork and exhaustion or in missed opportunities and unfulfilled potential.

Why 'coach yourself confident'?

Can we grow our confidence? Yes. Let's face it, it would be surprising if this wasn't my answer, given the title and premise of this book. I imagine that you know this too. There will be many examples of situations that used to trigger anxiety and fear in which you now feel confident. If you've learned to drive, it's unlikely that you felt confident with parallel parking from the outset. You might not love it now, but I'm willing to bet that you're more confident than you once were. This points to one of the ingredients of confidence that we'll come back to multiple times: practice.

Confidence is held in the thoughts we have about ourselves, and the emotions that those thoughts trigger. We can change our patterns of thinking; change the way we see ourselves. The wonder that is neuroplasticity means that we can literally rewire our brains. The ideas, stories and reflection activities in this book offer you the opportunity to look at your patterns of thinking, to explore the thoughts and beliefs that underpin your confidence and your self-doubt.

So, it's possible to grow your confidence. I believe that coaching offers one of the most effective ways to support that growth, and my intention is to offer the benefit of executive coaching within the pages of this book; coaching that's available on demand. The essence of coaching is that the coachee has the answers. Those answers might currently be out of reach, but they are there. The job of the coach is to support the coachee to explore their own thinking. Confidence is personal. It's about self-trust, something that only you can find. I don't have the answers, so I can't offer them to you. You know you from the inside. You have the capacity to grow your confidence, and the job of this book is to help you to access that capacity. My aim is to support you to find your confidence for yourself.

Doing the work

My invitation to you is to look inward and better understand how confidence and self-doubt show up for you. How it feels when you're at your most confident and how it feels when that sense of calm assurance eludes you. Together, we'll nurture your self-trust, growing a confidence that comes from within, a confidence which you can sustain despite the inevitable bumps and knocks that life brings. We'll explore and grow a sense of humble confidence that is in line with your capability. I invite you to get really curious, to approach the reading of this book as an enquiry into your confidence.

Within the pages to come, you'll read stories that I share in the hope that some of them will resonate with you, serving to shed light on your own experiences. The stories are drawn from my experiences as a coach; they are firmly based in reality, albeit the names and some details have been changed in order to protect anonymity.

Alongside the stories, you'll find shaded boxes scattered throughout the book, identifying activities for you to do. As a practical point, you might find it useful to have a notebook to hand in which you can complete the activities and capture your thoughts. The activities underpin what I believe to be the two key ingredients for growing confidence: awareness and practice. The reflection exercises (mirror icon) are activities designed to help you better understand your confidence. I encourage you to complete these as you go along, to build up your awareness of how your confidence (and self-doubt) works.

Why an emphasis on awareness? A thought that I frequently share with coaching clients is Tim Gallwey's suggestion that 'awareness is curative'. Gallwey is an author and coaching pioneer. His work translated some key ideas about high performance from the sporting sphere into the world of business. I find the idea of awareness being curative hugely encouraging. It's about turning inwards and understanding yourself, about really noticing what is true for you, and about trusting that this noticing will make a difference. That simply understanding more about ourselves triggers growth. At the core of the work to grow confidence is a deepening of your understanding of yourself. It requires you to excavate the layers of both your confidence and your self-doubt. If you feel a temptation to skip the reflection exercises, perhaps in a bid to speed through the book and find 'the answers', I implore you to resist that urge. Skipping those means skipping 80% of the work.

The second key ingredient for growing confidence is conscious practice, and you'll find many straightforward practices within the shaded boxes (leaf icon). These are tools to help you to access your confidence when you need it. You can try out these tools as you come to them in the book so that they become part of your toolkit, available to you as and when you need them. I know that these practices work because they have worked for me personally as I have grown my confidence over time, and I have seen the positive impact on my clients. These practices work, but that is not to say that they will all work for you. That is not a promise I can make because confidence is personal. There is no universal blueprint for building self-trust, and I think you should be highly sceptical about any offer of 'ten simple steps to confidence' or the like. I invite you to approach the *Coach Yourself Confident* practices with an open mind – try them out and find out what works for you.

I'm grateful that you've chosen to explore confidence – the fuel for life – with me.

Let's get started.

1

Fuel for life

We all have confidence. Without it we would struggle to meet the world on a daily basis. You might not have the deep well of confidence to which you aspire. You might be more intimately acquainted with your self-doubt than you are with your confidence. You might not feel able to access your confidence in the moments that you most need it. But your confidence is there. My hope is that reading this book will enable you to better acquaint yourself with your confidence, to find ways to access more easily what one of my interviewees described as 'feeling powerful from the inside', and to grow a fuller, more robust sense of what you're capable of.

In this chapter, we'll explore two questions. The first is: why grow our confidence? You will have your own story about what brought you here and what sits behind your aspiration to become more confident, and you'll intuitively know that confidence brings with it multiple benefits. My intention is to explore those benefits, and in doing so, solidify your desire to become more confident. We're more likely to really commit to a development goal if we have crystallized the benefits that we're seeking to gain, so this is useful foundational work. The second question is also fundamental: how do we grow confidence? This is important to understand at the outset, so that we can be intentional in how we go about strengthening our self-trust.

What does confidence give us?

Better odds

Confidence does not guarantee success, but it does stack the odds in our favour. There is truth in the words of Roman poet Virgil: 'Possunt quia posse videntur', which translates as 'they can because they think they can'. Or to use a slightly less highbrow reference, we can see the idea in the classic American children's story *The Little Engine That Could*. In the story, a train full of toys and food for the children on the other side of the mountain breaks down and several large engines refuse to help. The Little Blue Engine comes along, and although she is only small, she wants to help. 'Puff, puff, chug, chug, went the Little Blue Engine. "I think I can – I think I can – I think I can – I think I can – I think I can – I think I can – I think I can – I think I can – I think I can.'" Up and up she goes, faster and faster until she reaches the top of the mountain. As she begins to descend the other side, the Little Blue Engine says: 'I thought I could. I thought I could. I thought I could. I thought I could. I thought I could. I thought I could.' Just like the Little Blue Engine, our confidence is self-fulfilling: believing that we can do something increases the chances of success.

My own experience, and what I've observed in others during three decades in the world of work, tells me that confidence has a significant impact on performance at work. Imagine you're beginning the process of pulling together a strategy for your function. If you approach the task with 'I think I can' at the forefront of your mind, then you're likely to tackle it with energy and initiative. You might not have done anything similar before, but you trust yourself to work it out. You set up meetings to gain input, get hold of example strategy documents to gather ideas and start to sketch out some thoughts. Approaching the task with your head full of 'I can't do this' or 'this is going to be a disaster', on the other hand, would likely result in more tentative steps. It's difficult to get started, to invest the energy and hard work needed, when you hold the belief that the task is beyond you.

When Rebecca Snow, Global Human Resources (HR) Vice President for Mars Snacking, told me her confidence story, she was clear that for her, 'confidence makes a big, big performance difference.' As Rebecca talked to me about how she experiences confidence, what came through was the way that confidence enables her to fully demonstrate her strengths.

Rebecca experiences confidence as 'feeling powerful from the inside', which comes with a sense of stillness and a feeling of being 'centred'. From this place of composure and potency, she will vocalize her thoughts clearly and without undue hesitation, trusting that her perspective will add value. She feels a greater sense of ease in taking risks, making decisions and giving feedback. It is not that Rebecca stays silent, equivocates or holds back if her confidence dips – the difference is not that extreme – but her strengths are more muted. She may not share her perspective as quickly, as fully, as fluently. She may feel hesitant about weighing up risks and coming to a decision. She may be tempted to postpone a feedback conversation. Rebecca continues to perform well through the waxing and waning of her confidence, but the business gets the fullest version of Rebecca, her strengths in glorious technicolour, when she is lit by confidence from within.

The correlation between confidence and performance is evident in sport too. We can see that in the rise in prominence of psychologists as part of the coaching staff for a wide range of sports. When I spoke to Kate Richardson-Walsh, captain of the Olympic gold medal winning hockey team and most capped female hockey player for Great Britain, she told me that confidence was '*the* thing', saying 'it was the hardest thing to get, the hardest thing to talk about, the hardest thing to get our heads around. But I think that the people who had an ability to maintain their confidence for longer or were able to get through the low confidence bits, those were the people who tended to be consistently performing at the top. They were the ones who were selected more often than not. It was all about confidence.'

The connection between a positive mindset (aka confidence) and sporting success is widely understood. There is much that we can learn from the world of sport; lessons that apply in the business setting and can help us to perform to our full potential. In his book, *The Inner Game of Tennis*, Tim Gallwey says: 'The biggest opponent is on your own side of the net.'[2] The inner game is 'the game that takes place in the mind of the player, and it is played against such obstacles as lapses in concentration, nervousness, self-doubt and self-condemnation.'[3] Gallwey refers to these internal obstacles as 'interference' and sets out a simple equation to illustrate its impact:

Performance = potential − interference[4]

Simply, the lower the interference, the better the odds of success. Thinking 'oh no, it's coming to my backhand, that's my weakness' will inevitably undermine your ability to hit a good return. Similarly, beating yourself up mid-game with 'you idiot, how did you send that out?' undermines your ability to play your best tennis. Worrying about how well you're playing makes it more difficult for you to play well. This is true at any level of the game; Rafael Nadal, one of the greatest players in history says: 'What I battle hardest to do in a tennis match is to quiet the voices in my head.'[5] Whenever I talk to leaders about the inner game, I ask if the idea that we are our own biggest opponent resonates with their own experience of playing sport. The answer is always a resounding yes. I hear stories of the connection between decreasing shot accuracy and increasing frustration on the golf course making the 18 holes a miserable experience. I

---

[2] Gallwey, 1986.

[3] Gallwey, 1986.

[4] Gallwey, 1998.

[5] Kross, 2021.

hear cyclists who are only too aware of how the story they tell themselves directly influences their race times, either positively or negatively.

The formula *performance* = *potential* – *interference* holds true as much in business as it does in sport. Self-doubt voiced by our inner critic can knock us off our game. We're in conversation, and at the same time we're observing ourselves in that conversation and having a silent dialogue with ourselves. *Did I say that clearly? Do they think I'm an idiot?* These thoughts clutter our mind and diminish our ability to bring our full selves, and all of our knowledge and thinking, to the conversation. Worrying about how well we're coming across makes it more difficult for us to come across well.

In contrast, accessing your confidence enables you to quieten the voices of self-doubt and self-condemnation, clearing your mind of interference. Now you are better able to draw on all of your resources in that work conversation. Confidence unlocks a state of calm focus that we might call 'being in the zone' or 'being in flow'. Many interviewees during my research for this book referenced this state in some way. Their descriptions of confidence included the phrase 'it feels like being centred', as well as the words 'grounded' and 'balanced'. One interviewee talked about 'being able to breathe'. Matt Ridsdale, Group Chief Corporate Affairs Officer at the media and entertainment company, Sky, acknowledged the joy of having minimal mental interference: 'I think that confidence gives me quite a strong sense of contentment. Others who perhaps have less confidence might look at what I've been tasked with doing in my various roles and wonder how on earth I sleep. They would be riddled with anxiety in a way that I am not. That's a bit of a privilege.'

COACH YOURSELF CONFIDENT #1

 REFLECTION: Better odds

The intention of this short exercise is for you to reflect on the way in which your confidence positively impacts your performance.

Bring to mind a recent situation in which you felt confident. Try to inhabit that situation again, imagine that you are back there:

- Where are you, who is there, what is happening?
- What are you thinking or saying to yourself?

Now think about:

- What is it about the situation that underpins your feeling of confidence?
  - What's present?
  - What's absent?

- How does your feeling of confidence show itself?
  - What is the feeling that you notice?
  - How would you describe your confidence?

- What does this confidence enable?
  - Can you make any connections between your feeling of confidence and your performance in the situation?

A willingness to say YES

When we're faced with the opportunity to do something new, we have no way of knowing whether or not we can do that new thing unless we say yes. We can't expand our comfort zone, the home territory where we feel at ease, unless we move towards new challenges and take on things that provoke fear. Saying yes allows us to stretch ourselves, and confidence makes it easier to say yes. I want to share a story about having the confidence to say yes.

White Swan is a UK charity that uses technology to accelerate diagnosis and improve treatment for individuals with long-term, undiagnosed conditions. Set up in 2016, White Swan was initially a not-for-profit arm of Black Swan Data Limited, later becoming an independent registered charity. The charity was born out of the experience of Steve King, Black Swan's co-founder and Chief Executive Officer (CEO). Steve's sister, Julie, had significant, undiagnosed health problems, and by 2015, ten years of deteriorating health had left her in a wheelchair. Doctors told her family to prepare for the worst, but Steve refused to accept his sister's bleak prognosis. Having understood the power of predictive analytics to find patterns and connections that would be impossible for a single human being to spot, he set out to apply the same techniques to help his sister. Using Black Swan's technology, Steve and his team helped clinicians to diagnose his sister with a rare form of Parkinson's disease. Effective treatment was quickly initiated and Julie began to make an astonishing recovery. The idea for White Swan was born.

How to make that idea a reality? Steve turned to his friend Miranda Mapleton and asked if she would establish the charity.

The starting brief was simply to use Black Swan's technology for good; the blankest of blank sheets of paper. So what was it that equipped Miranda to take on the role and to successfully build a charity that today partners with well-known charities, big pharmaceutical businesses and the leading hospitals in the UK? Miranda is a talented marketer who has led teams in global businesses including PepsiCo, Mars and Miele. Known for her sharp strategic mind and her ability to make things happen, Miranda has left a lasting legacy on the brands that she has led. Her impressive marketing CV was not the obvious background for a charity CEO.

Miranda described the experience of founding and building White Swan as 'without a doubt the hardest thing I've ever done in my career.' Establishing the charity meant heading into uncharted territory and figuring things out as she went. New to technology, new to medicine, new to the charity sector, and with no structure in which to operate, there was an enormous amount for Miranda to learn. 'Confidence came from knowing that I'd done other things. But it didn't tell me I could do this thing,' she told me. Making such a significant career pivot meant that Miranda wasn't doing more of the same, she wasn't deploying the marketing expertise that she had built over the years. Instead, she was taking the evidence of her capability and choosing to apply that capability in a very different setting. She was able to recognize that she possessed the fundamentals of what she would need, telling herself, 'I know I can think. I've got a good brain here. I can do these different things I haven't done before.'

Miranda knew that her ability to think her way through things would apply just as much to the process of building a charity as it had done to the process of building a brand.

This ingredient of her confidence was portable from one context to another, but a good brain was not the only thing that would be needed; it would take much more than that to ensure the success of White Swan. Seeing where she would need to supplement her own skills, experience and ability to figure things out, Miranda forged relationships, inspired others to get involved and approached people in her network for support. I asked Miranda if she'd had moments when she wondered what the hell she was doing as the CEO of a charity, if she'd ever had a sneaking suspicion that somehow there had been an error, that she wasn't equipped for the role? That perhaps she'd said yes when it might have been better to say no? Her answer was refreshingly clear: no.

I shared Matt Ridsdale's reflection on minimal mental interference a few pages ago, and I'd like to share a little more from my interview with Matt as we consider the way that confidence enables us to say yes. I worked alongside Matt during his time at Camelot (the operator of the UK's national lottery) and he had always struck me as being a person who exuded a warm and natural self-confidence. As I began my book research, I was keen to talk to him because I wanted to find out whether my perception was accurate – did the confidence I observed exist on the inside? That was my first question, and the answer was yes. I asked Matt what that confidence brings with it and he told me, 'you get to do more things because you just say yes to pretty much everything.' Matt has amassed an impressive array of experiences as a result of saying yes. Those experiences have brought with them a broad perspective, an extensive network and some fantastic stories. This one is from Matt's time at a communications agency.

'We got a brief from a client to work with him and the Clinton Global Initiative to respond to the aftermath of the earthquake in Haiti. It was quite dangerous, and the insurance company wasn't thrilled about it. Everyone in the firm said, "you must be joking" – apart from me.' So off Matt went, arriving in Haiti with a briefcase and a desire to help. He didn't take directly relevant experience with him, having never worked on relief efforts in the wake of an earthquake. What he took was curiosity and a willingness to embrace the new. 'I know that sort of sounds ridiculous – that I turned up on my own with my briefcase – but at the time, it just wasn't remotely ridiculous. I just thought that sounds so interesting. And if we can help, that'd be great. I don't know how much of a difference it'll make, but it's worth trying. Everything was worth a go.'

Confidence enables us to say yes to the full panoply of wonder, excitement, horror, uncertainty and fabulous craziness that life has to offer.

The trust of others

Research suggests that we mix up confidence and competence. That's good news for those with bags of confidence, but bad news for those of us whose bags are replete with self-doubt. We make an assumption that someone who speaks and acts with confidence must know what they are doing. We place our trust in the confident doctor; we are unnerved by the doctor who appears to lack conviction. In simulated job interviews, confidence has been found to be a more successful strategy than modesty,[6] and people making stock

---

[6] Tenney and Spellman, 2010.

market choices have been shown to prefer confident financial advisors.[7] Confidence is contagious. If we are confident in ourselves, then others are more likely to trust in our abilities.

In my research interviews, this *confidence = competence* assumption came up most strongly in my conversation with Si Bradley, a former Colonel in the British Army. Si gave an example of *confidence = competence* in action: 'I've worked with some great, great leaders who I've seen exude confidence. And that has made me feel more confident, even before I've been asked to do anything. It all boils down to a confident presence. I have, within two minutes of meeting someone, thought to myself, I don't even know what you're going to ask me to do, but I'm going to do it because I have the confidence in your ability to operate and think at this level.' There's another layer to highlight in Si's example, something else that contributes to his willingness to believe that the confidence of the officer in front of him is an accurate reflection of their capability. Si trusted the system; he trusted the soundness of the British Army's system for training and appointing officers. When he met Army colleagues at any rank, those individuals did not need to prove their capability because Si started with an assumption that they were there because they were competent.

A collective power

There's another form of confidence contagion, one which sparks a collective power in teams. This contagion is when seeing your confidence leads me to feel more confident in

---

[7] Price and Stone, 2004.

myself: 'If *you* feel confident in this thing we're about to do together, then *I* feel confident too.' We've already looked at how confidence can increase our odds of individual success, so it's easy to imagine how this multiplying up of confidence can be transformative for a team. Olympian Kate Richardson-Walsh told me about the way in which confidence was contagious within the Great Britain hockey team. Part of their preparation for the Rio Olympics in 2016 was for each team member to identify and share their 'super strengths' – the unique skills and attributes that they brought to the team. Each individual's super strengths formed the foundation for their confidence, and the process of sharing brought all of that confidence together, reinforcing and growing a shared belief that the team could succeed. Kate described the impact: 'There was a steely knowledge that we're bringing all these different strengths to the table in this group. So whatever the Olympics threw at us, and we knew it was going to throw us some curveballs, we'd be able to find a way to win because of this collective strength. That's powerful.'

Confidence contagion can work in reverse too, sapping confidence within a team. Kate had seen this earlier in her career: 'When there's a lot of doubt about team and individual performance, that can absolutely light a fire. And if you get a critical mass of team members thinking we can't win this game today, then there's absolutely no way you're going to win it. It impacts your thoughts, your words, your actions, it affects everything.' This is a case of collective self-doubt worsening the odds of success.

Ben Lamont, Senior HR Director at Kellanova, described to me how team confidence contagion can work in a business setting. Ben's style is characterized by a natural positivity and optimism, and he sees the confidence boosting impact that this can have on his colleagues. Ben actively uses this understanding to cultivate confidence, energy and momentum within his team. 'I've often found myself saying, "I haven't got a clue how we're going to do this, but I know it can be done, and I know we'll find a way."' Ben draws confidence from the previous times when he and the team were tasked with something new and challenging, and successfully found a way through. 'I have to believe that we'll achieve what we're being asked to do, even if it's in entirely unknown territory, and I have to exude that belief. As a leader, you need that belief, that faith, and it helps the team to believe.'

The difference for you

The next *Coach Yourself Confident* activity is an opportunity to sharpen up your aspiration in relation to confidence, enabling you to approach the book with clarity about what you're hoping to gain. It's an invitation to note down your thoughts on your current relationship with confidence – when can you access it with ease, when does it elude you? And it's an invitation to set out what a greater level of confidence would look and feel like for you. Later in the book, I'll be inviting you to return to the notes that you make here. You can consider this as your best current thinking on where you're headed on your confidence adventure. As you read the coming chapters, you will likely refine your thinking about where you're heading, and you'll get clear on the steps that you can take to get there.

COACH YOURSELF CONFIDENT #2

 REFLECTION: Your confidence aspiration

Part 1: Confidence baseline

In what situations do you feel at your most confident?

- Note down the situations that come to mind, and then see if you can identify any themes about what bolsters your confidence.

In what situations are you aware of a lack of confidence?

- Again, note down the situations and then look for themes, this time about what diminishes your confidence.

Part 2: Confidence aspiration

What is your aspiration in relation to confidence?

- What is the shift that you'd like to make?
- What would be different for you, and how would that feel?
- What would others see and hear?

How do we grow confidence?

So, there are compelling reasons why we would want to build our confidence: it can improve our performance, enable us to step forward more easily and take on new opportunities, lead others to trust in our abilities and fuel our collaborative endeavours. You may well have identified more personal reasons too, as you crystallized what you hope to gain from coaching yourself confident. So how do we go about accessing those benefits? To start to answer that question, we need to get under the skin of how confidence works.

The momentum of confidence

I asked to interview Chris Fawkes, a weather forecaster and presenter, because I was holding a hypothesis that it must take enormous confidence to broadcast live to millions of people in the UK and around the world on the BBC and the BBC World Service. I thought that perhaps the conversation might unearth a secret to confidence that I could share with you. It was a fascinating conversation, and it did uncover some important points about confidence, although they may be more prosaic than I had hoped. Perhaps I shouldn't have been surprised that Chris's confidence works in pretty much the same way as everyone else's, despite the fact that his work is much more visible than is likely to be the case for the rest of us.

Let me start with the reason why I thought that Chris must possess a special kind of confidence by setting out a quick summary of what he does. After analysing a mind-boggling amount of data in order to figure out what's happening with the weather in different parts of the globe, Chris prepares to present the forecast in a short segment of a few minutes, either on TV or radio. He has to communicate the complexities of the weather forecast in an easily understandable way for the viewers and listeners, ensuring that he covers all of the key points and doesn't forget any geographies. During his broadcast, Chris will have a producer's voice in his ear, and they may tell him mid-segment that he has 20 seconds less than he expected, or perhaps 30 seconds more. For this reason, it's impossible to prepare a script so the forecast he gives is all ad lib. In Chris's words, the experience is 'quite intense' and he has 'quite a lot of information sort of sloshing around' in his mind. And let's not forget that Chris broadcasts live, and that his work is viewed or heard by millions of people.

To me, Chris's job sounds more than 'quite intense' – it sounds terrifying. If I were to give it a go of course it would be terrifying because I'd be a complete beginner attempting to do a very specialist job. What's easy to miss is that tens of thousands of hours of hard work and practice have contributed to Chris's ability as a weather presenter. During that time, he has built his skill, he has built up a tolerance for the intensity, and he has grown in confidence. Core to that process has been experience, or to put it another way, practice. What was difficult and nerve-wracking to begin with has become normal as the result of repeated effort and finding out what works (and what doesn't). 'I don't tend to get nervous now, but I've been broadcasting for over two decades. Have I ever felt nervous? Absolutely. If I think back to my first bit of TV experience on local TV channels, you bet I was nervous. I think that passes, and I think it's down to experience – you just keep doing it.'

Chris is talking about the idea of confidence momentum. You take action, choosing to do something even if it's scary. Then you gain data as a result of experience – you learn what works and what doesn't, drawing insight from both progress and setback. Through practice, hard work and perseverance, what might seem inordinately difficult to someone else (and perhaps also to you at the outset) becomes part of your comfort zone. Chris summarized this aspect of growing confidence succinctly: 'If you push yourself to do something that's uncomfortable, it becomes comfortable after a while.' I think this really helps us to answer our question about how we can grow confidence.

I see it as a cycle:

THE CONFIDENCE MOMENTUM CYCLE

It starts with taking action: we try something and we see what happens. Taking an intention and converting it into an action provides us with data – did our action have the impact that we anticipated? The learnings might lead us to correct our course (we go round the setback loop and try again). Or we might learn that our action took us closer to our goal, which adds to our trust in ourselves and makes it easier to keep trying – continuing around the loop. As we build momentum, it can become easier to step forward and act. Whereas the setback loop might initially feel uncomfortable, with intentional practice, we can begin to see setbacks as both inevitable and useful. The Confidence Momentum Cycle represents a virtuous circle as we gain evidence of what we are capable of, which in turn builds our confidence and motivation to act. And the momentum of the *action – learn – progress – confidence* loop fuels success because simply the act of taking action makes success more likely. Confidence fuels progress and progress fuels confidence.

If it were easy to gain and maintain this momentum of confidence, then this would be a very short book. The message would be simple and straightforward: take action. This is good advice in that action can fuel confidence, and inaction can fuel self-doubt, but it's not enough. There are a number of potential interruptions to this cycle that we need to consider, which we'll explore in more depth in the upcoming chapters.

The first interruption comes right up front: you listen to the doubts articulated by your inner critic and choose not to act. When this happens, fear robs you of possibility; it robs you of the learning you could gain and it robs you of the progress you might make if only you gave it a try. A delay between choosing to act and the moment of taking action can be seen as an invitation to your inner critic. They might step in to fill the lull with messages of self-sabotage that make it increasingly difficult to take the plunge. My fellow coach, Mark Chamberlen, experienced this kind of battle with his inner critic a few months ago during a period of limbo between agreeing a significant piece of work with a new client and that piece of work beginning. The wait for the green light was disorienting and uncomfortable as Mark's inner critic questioned his capability. 'Once I got started, I got that mojo back, I got that confidence.' It was Mark who made the connection between confidence and momentum, and in doing so, triggered me to sketch out the cycle.

The second interruption is a distortion of the setback loop. Instead of the setback loop as shown here – you use what you learn to enable you to correct your course and try again – the learn step becomes dominated by 'learnings' about how useless you are. You dwell on the setback and see it not as useful data to help you reshape the way forward, but as an evaluation of your ability. *I should have thought it through better, what an idiot.* Or *maybe this is just beyond me, I can't do it.* It can be tempting to shrink back – *I tried it and it didn't work.* This is the inner critic at work again. You won't be surprised to hear that the inner critic gets a fair bit of attention within the pages of this book, with the aim of shining a light on how they work and playing with ways to quieten the volume on their undermining narrative. We'll also explore some specific ideas about overcoming setbacks as part of Chapter 6.

A third potential interruption is when progress does not translate into a growth in confidence. You take action, and your action delivers the anticipated outcome, moving you forward towards your goal. But this experience doesn't increase your self-confidence. Perhaps you attribute the progress to luck, or to the actions of others. Or perhaps you minimize it in your mind, telling yourself that it was easy and anyone could have done it. These internal responses prevent you from seeing the progress as evidence of what you can do, so your view of your capability remains unchanged. This is the territory of faulty calibration, which we'll come to in Chapter 4.

Feeling the fear and doing it anyway

Let's look straightaway at that first potential interruption: fear. Instead of stepping forward and taking action, fear and self-doubt leads us to step back. There's a paradox that in order to build confidence, we must push ourselves to take action without it. It's the repeated experience of acting, learning and progressing – in spite of our self-doubt – that grows our confidence over time. Susan Jeffers nailed it with the title of her classic book written in 1987, *Feel the Fear and Do it Anyway*. Fear is a critical element in the process of building confidence. By pushing ourselves to do something new and scary, we find out a bit more about what we're capable of. We do it once and we survive. We find that perhaps we can add that new, scary thing to the range of situations that we're comfortable in. It might not be immediate – it may well take more than one try before we get comfortable – but if we keep pushing ourselves eventually it becomes less scary. We might even start to enjoy it. Our confidence has grown.

Stef Reid is an exceptional athlete, a multiple paralympic medallist and a world champion. Stef embraces the opportunity to do new and different things. Since retiring from competitive athletics, Stef has begun a career in broadcasting, qualified as an executive coach and taken up ice-skating after falling in love with the sport as a competitor on the TV programme Dancing on Ice. On a recent podcast, Stef reflected: 'I have self-doubt all the time, but I guess in some ways I don't necessarily see it as a negative thing. If I'm given an opportunity, or someone asks me to do something, and the first thing that I feel is fear and self-doubt, for me that is a trigger… that is something you must do! Or that it's something you at least need to explore because I know that it's something that's going to stretch me, it's going to make me uncomfortable. And that's a good thing.'[8]

What enables Stef to take action, even if she doubts herself, is a commitment to keep stretching herself. Her passion for learning and growing outweighs the fear of getting it wrong. She says: 'You have to find a way to be really OK with looking foolish and you kind of just have to leave your pride at the door. Be OK with being the person who asks the stupid questions and not caring in the moment how silly you look but seeing that in the future, two days from now, I'm going to look really smart when I get this right.'[9] Stef's philosophy seems to be 'I won't be good at a new thing straightaway, and that's OK. I'll put in the work and improve.' Stef has a deep confidence in her ability to learn, and that's what enables her to take action; to feel the fear and do it anyway.

When I explored the topic of confidence with former professional dancer Sarah Dickens, what stood out to me was the sheer bloody-minded determination that enabled her to take action, and to keep taking action despite setbacks. Sarah began dancing before she started school and decided early on that she wanted to pursue a career in the theatre. After dance college and a number of years performing on cruise ships, Sarah began to audition for the top theatre shows. What

---

[8] Humphries and Hughes, The High Performance Podcast Episode 174 – Stef Reid (23 January 2023).

[9] See note 8.

Sarah lacked in self-confidence, she made up for in grit. Her first big theatre role was Starlight Express in Germany, an Andrew Lloyd Webber musical in which a child's train set magically comes to life and the various engines compete to become the fastest in the world. An incredibly fast-moving show with the dancers flying around a racetrack on roller skates, the show elicited more than the usual level of nerves.

'I don't think I've ever done anything so scary in my life. I can dance, I can sing, I can act. But skating?! I've got eight wheels on my feet and every bit of dance technique I've learned since I was four years old is just out the window.' There was an enormous amount to learn. By the end of the four months of rehearsals, Sarah had no toenails, a chipped cheekbone and a new skill – she could skate. During that tough four months, there were numerous times when Sarah called home in tears. But when her mum suggested that Sarah come home, the answer was immediate. No. Sarah knew that if she went home she would always regret it. She knew that getting through this would bring an enormous sense of achievement and she wasn't about to give up. 'If I've said I'll do something, I'm doing it. If I can't do it, I'll work hard until I can do it.'

Sarah's formula started with setting an ambitious goal. Her passion for the goal kept her going, combined with a willingness to work hard and an absolute aversion to quitting. This was how she was able to take action and keep taking action, however tough the experience. Set a goal. Feel the fear and do it anyway. Keep going. Don't quit. Achievement follows, and with it comes confidence. I like this line from Roy T. Bennett's book *The Light in the Heart*: 'Don't be pushed around by the fears in your mind. Be led by the dreams in your heart.' It feels apt for both Stef and Sarah: their passion outweighs their fear.

COACH YOURSELF CONFIDENT #3

 REFLECTION: Feeling the fear and doing it anyway

Can you think of situations in which you felt the fear and did it anyway? Times when you were aware of self-doubt, and you took action regardless?

What was it that enabled you to take action in spite of your self-doubt? Perhaps you can identify the formula that helps you to maintain the circle of momentum that grows confidence?

To sum up...

- Confidence doesn't guarantee success, but it does stack the odds in our favour. Approaching a task with a belief that we can do it increases the likelihood that we'll be able to.

- Confidence enables us to step forward and seize opportunities; it helps us to say yes.

- Confidence is contagious; if we are confident in ourselves, then others are more likely to trust in our abilities. Confidence contagion happens in teams too, increasing the chances of team success.

- Confidence fuels progress and progress fuels confidence. It's a virtuous circle as we gain evidence of what we are capable of, which in turn builds our confidence and motivation to continue to take steps forward. This is the Confidence Momentum Cycle.

- The paradox is that in order to build confidence, we must push ourselves to take action without it; we must find a way to move forward despite our self-doubt. Feel the fear and do it anyway.

2

The self-doubt tax

In the first chapter, we explored what you stand to gain by growing your confidence, looking at the relationship between confidence and performance, the opportunities that it can open up for us, and the way that trusting ourselves leads others to trust us. Whilst these benefits are significant, I imagine that the desire to grasp them is only part of the reason why you have this book in your hands. As someone whose confidence lags behind your capability, you will be only too aware of the downsides that are associated with an excess of self-doubt. The process of unlocking humble confidence is as much about leaving these downsides behind as it is about moving towards the benefits of confidence. This chapter zeroes in on self-doubt, supporting you to reflect on how it plays out for you and offering you some practical tools to keep it in check.

Whilst self-doubt is a normal, unavoidable and in some ways useful part of the human experience, an excess of self-doubt is a heavy weight to carry. 'Self-doubt tax' is the way that I describe the impact of carrying the heavy weight of over-sized self-doubt. It's the cost of giving too much power to our self-doubt, of unquestioningly believing our inner critic. Too many of us pay this tax, and it's levied in two ways:

TWO FORMS OF SELF-DOUBT TAX

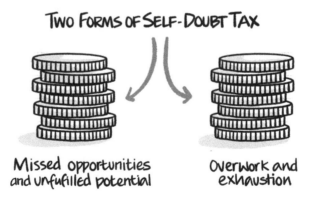

Missed opportunities
and unfufilled potential

Overwork and
exhaustion

When we allow our confidence to hold us back, we stay small and safe, paying the self-doubt tax in the form of missed opportunities and unfulfilled potential. When we push ourselves to achieve impressive results despite a nagging self-doubt, we pay the tax in the form of overwork and exhaustion with self-defeating habits such as over preparation and punishingly high standards. These two forms of the self-doubt tax are not mutually exclusive; it is not a case of one or the other – the self-doubt taxman is sneakier than that.

The dictionary tells me that a tax is 'a compulsory contribution to state revenue, levied by the government.' The thing about the self-doubt tax is that it's voluntary, not compulsory. For as long as we allow our confidence to lag behind our capability, then we are choosing to pay the self-doubt tax. I realize that this may be difficult to accept because it won't feel like a tax contribution that you're making willingly, but the fact that it's voluntary is key. If the self-doubt tax is voluntary and you choose to pay it, then you can choose *not* to pay it by reducing your level of self-doubt. It's only when your self-doubt is over-sized that a self-doubt tax payment is due.

My invitation to you in the pages to come is to quantify the self-doubt tax that you are paying, and to begin to experiment with ways to right-size your self-doubt and thereby lower your self-doubt tax burden. The aim is that ultimately you can stop paying the tax altogether.

How self-doubt shows up

First things first, how does self-doubt show up? We'll start by exploring the ways that self-doubt is evident in what we tell ourselves and in what we say to others.

The inner critic

I'd suggest that one of the things that unites those of us who wish to increase our confidence is that our inner critic is particularly loud, is not easily dissuaded from sharing a view and is all too often painfully present. The inner critic is trying to be a friend, trying to keep us safe. It wants to help us avoid doing something wrong, either in our eyes or in the eyes of others. Whilst its intention is good, its over vigilance leads it to be a loud and diminishing presence. My inner critic is incredibly committed and hard working. He (for me, it's a 'he') is alert to any signal that I've done something wrong, or that I might be about to do something wrong. And for him, 'wrong' has a very wide-ranging definition. From decades of experience in supporting others to be effective at work, I know that I am amongst good company as the owner of a very active inner critic.

The alertness of the inner critic provokes a self-consciousness that disconnects us from the present moment. We are in a meeting, sitting at a table with colleagues, participating in a conversation. Physically we are at the table, but our inner critic is hovering above, observing and monitoring, evaluating and checking. It's impossible to be fully ourselves, to just say what we want to say, when our inner critic is chattering away. *If you say that, you'll look like an idiot.* Now you're worrying not only about the content of the conversation, but about the outcome of an imagined process of performance appraisal.

In its ill-informed attempt to keep us safe, our inner critic focuses on risk, so it's particularly alert to any kind of deficiency. It's not interested in what works well for us, what capabilities we have, our shining strengths. Instead its focus is on what's not working, what we lack, what we haven't done. As a consequence, the owners of a harsh inner critic can find it hard, or well-nigh impossible, to take full credit for their achievements or full ownership of their strengths. Think about what happens when a colleague praises you. Do you say something like 'thank you, it took a lot of hard work and focus. I'm really pleased and I think what I've delivered will make a real difference.' Or something more like 'it was nothing, just doing my job' or 'you would have done it just as well' or 'it was all a matter of luck really – just happened to be right place, right time.' If you can hear yourself saying any of these three latter phrases, that's your inner critic speaking, distancing you from your accomplishment because success doesn't fit with the inner critic's well-established narrative.

Ironically, you might feel that your inner critic is vastly overconfident. They don't hesitate in their judgement and are strongly attached to the 'I told you so' narrative, meaning that you ignore them at your peril. If you take a deep breath and act despite your nerves, your inner critic will be ready to jump on any shred of evidence to suggest that this was a bad idea: *See – I was right. I warned you that this was a bad idea, that you'd look like a fool.* Or as you gather your courage to act, they might whisper: *Remember last time you ignored me, it didn't go so well, did it?*

Our inner critics are as unique as we are, but there are some common inner critic strategies. See if any of these resonate for you.

- I keep you safe by reminding you to maintain exceptionally high standards. Be perfect.
- I keep you safe by reminding you to put the needs and wants of others ahead of your own needs. Please others.
- I keep you safe by reminding you that your worth is measured by the pace and volume of your work. Go faster. Work harder.

- I keep you safe by reminding you that failure is not an option. Do it brilliantly. Or don't do it at all. Don't fail.
- I keep you safe by reminding you that asking for help makes you look weak. You need to work it out yourself. Be strong.

Your inner critic might use a blend of these strategies, which I've based on the 1975 work of Taibi Kahler.[10] A combination of 'be perfect' and 'work harder' can be particularly exhausting. A combination of 'be perfect' and 'please others' can lead us to tie ourselves in knots on a piece of work as we seek to line up what others want with our own view of what perfect looks like. With the next reflection activity, I invite you to unmask your inner critic.

COACH YOURSELF CONFIDENT #4

 REFLECTION: Unmask your inner critic

Your inner critic is at its most powerful when it operates in the shadows. This unmasking exercise is designed to shine a light on them, and in doing so, to lessen their power.

Step 1: Hearing your inner critic

What does your inner critic have to say? What are the messages that you frequently hear? A couple of my inner critic's favourite lines are: *You sound like an idiot!* and *I thought you were supposed to be good at this!*

---

[10] Stewart and Joines, 1987.

Step 2: Seeing your inner critic

Now take a moment to imagine your inner critic. What does it look like? A person, a monster, an animal, an object? Large, small? Colourful, drab? Draw a picture of it. I know that this sounds like a strange thing to do, but it can be really powerful, so I encourage you to give it a try.

Note: Watch out for your inner critic having an opinion on your picture! If you'd find it helpful to have some inspiration (or to give yourself permission to transfer the image that's in your mind onto paper), you could take a look at the online gallery of inner critic pictures that coach, artist, writer and speaker, Steve Chapman has created. You can find it at: https://innercriticexperiment.tumblr.com

Once you've drawn your own inner critic, you could add it to Steve's gallery.

We can put distance between the harsh commentary of our inner critic and our sense of self. It's when we absorb what our inner critic tells us that our confidence is undermined, so gaining some distance from what our inner critic has to say lessens their power. It's this idea of distance that underpins the 'unmask your inner critic' activity above. Now I'd like to offer you four more ways to remind yourself that your inner critic is not you. Your thoughts are separate from who you are, and you don't have to believe what your inner critic tells you.

COACH YOURSELF CONFIDENT #5

 PRACTICE: Keep your distance

Name your inner critic

Giving your inner critic a name underlines the separation between your inner critic and who you are.

Old Nigel is off again, telling me that I'm not up to the job.

Make a note

Try to write down what your inner critic is telling you verbatim – capture the words that you hear in your mind. Written down, the harshness of your inner critic becomes even more apparent. You see the exaggeration, and sometimes just reading it back is enough to loosen the inner critic's hold in that particular moment.

Keeping a journal can be helpful too. It provides an opportunity to observe your emotions and thoughts, and to notice patterns over time.

Say thank you

When you notice that your inner critic is active, acknowledge its good intentions. Thank it for trying to look after you and explain the choice that you are making.

Thank you for trying to keep me safe – I hear that you think that speaking in this meeting is risky, but I'm choosing to share my point of view now.

Fool your inner critic

In her book *The Rise*, Sarah Lewis recounts a Paris Review interview with the playwright August Wilson. A waitress at a café frequented by Wilson noticed that he often wrote on a paper napkin. She asked him if he wrote on napkins because it doesn't count. The playwright said: 'If I pull out a tablet, I'm saying "now I'm writing", and I become more conscious of being a writer.' His napkin became a safe haven, a way of silencing the inner critic before it was time for it to have its say.[11] Perhaps you could think of what an equivalent practice might be for you – a low stakes way of getting started on a piece of work that feels big and scary.

Words that sow the seeds of doubt

'Language is very powerful. Language does not just describe reality. Language creates the reality it describes.' (Desmond Tutu, South African Anglican archbishop and winner of the Nobel Peace Prize). If we tell ourselves we can't, we'll start to believe it. We must watch what we tell ourselves silently in the privacy of our own minds, and we must be mindful

[11] Lewis, 2015.

about the words we choose when we express ourselves to others. The language that we use impacts how we feel about ourselves as well as how others see us. Our choice of words can diminish or build confidence in our own eyes, and in the eyes of those around us.

We all have catchphrases, the automatic things that we say without really thinking. It's possible that you have a catchphrase (or two) that signal a lack of confidence. In Chapter 1, we saw how confidence is contagious, that we tend to trust people who appear confident. The opposite also holds true: we are more likely to doubt the abilities of a person who seems to doubt themselves. A tone that's quiet and tentative, or sentences that are filled with caveats, disclaimers and apologies; these all convey a lack of trust in yourself. How many of these phrases can you hear yourself saying?

- 'You've probably thought of this already…'
- 'It's only half an idea, but…'
- 'More than likely, this won't work…'
- '… anyway, it's just a thought, it's probably not helpful.'

Questions can convey a lack of confidence too. The subtext behind the question 'Does that make sense?' is not 'Is the point of view I have articulated clear to you? Do you have questions?' but 'Please can you assuage my doubt and reassure me that I have said something worthwhile?' More confident alternatives to experiment with include: 'What do you make of that?', 'Do you have any questions so far?' and 'Any reflections on that?'

Another verbal signal of self-doubt is the unnecessary apology. For example, someone asks you a question during a presentation and you respond with 'Apologies, I obviously did not make that clear' or 'Sorry, I really should have said that up front.' During a conversation, a thoughtful expression on your colleague's face is met with 'Sorry, I'm waffling aren't I?' (Both an unnecessary apology and a request for reassurance.) It's an auto-response based on an assumption that *it must be my fault.* Or you might hear yourself say 'Sorry, but I don't think I agree with that.' Are you sorry? Do you need to be sorry for having a different point of view, or is this an auto-response based on a need to be liked by others? If you're a compulsive apologizer, you could try keeping a tally of the number of times you say 'sorry' during a day. It might be useful to ask a colleague to help you keep track – if it's an automatic habit, you might not notice you're doing it. If it seems like a high tally of unnecessary apologies, experiment with a 'no sorry meeting' or a 'no sorry day' to see if you can interrupt the urge to apologize.

Self-doubt sometimes comes packaged as a self-deprecating joke: 'Ha, I'm such an idiot!' And this kind of joke can also be a buy-one-get-one-free with an unnecessary apology: 'Aargh! sorry for talking absolute drivel. My brain is such mush.' It might be enlightening to start keeping a note of the 'jokes' that you make about yourself. Again, you might want to ask a colleague to help raise your awareness by letting you know when you do it. After a week or two, have a look through what you've noted down and be strict with yourself. Are you really an idiot? Is your brain really mush?

COACH YOURSELF CONFIDENT #6

 REFLECTION: Mind your language

Spoken

Try doing an audit of your spoken language, looking out for phrases and habits that appear regularly when you speak, and that could have the effect of shining a light on your self-doubt. You could record some conversations (with permission from the other participants) or perhaps ask a trusted colleague to listen carefully and play back what they notice about your verbal habits.

Email

A quick (and potentially revealing) experiment is to take a look back at the emails you have sent over the last few days and analyse the language you have used. Are your emails peppered with *just, maybe, perhaps, a little, might, possibly*? If so, do these words support your message? Do they represent a conscious choice of tone on your behalf – signs of a polite and professional approach – or do they represent a habit that conveys a lack of confidence?

Watch out for language that unintentionally communicates messages such as:

- I'm not really sure what I think.
- It's probably a stupid idea anyway.

- I don't really expect you to do what I ask.
- I'm inconveniencing you.
- What I say doesn't really matter.

You could continue the experiment with an extra layer of awareness as you compose emails during the week ahead. Scan your wording before you press send and play with editing out the 'justs' and 'maybes'. How does it read now? Still you? More confident?

Important note: I've suggested that you look out for your language habits, both in email and out loud. There's a risk that this triggers you to beat yourself up. I'd encourage you to approach this awareness exercise in a spirit of curiosity rather than evaluation. It's about noticing patterns and spotting small changes that you could make. It's not about marking yourself out of ten. Remember: awareness is curative.

Nerves and butterflies

Nerves. Butterflies. Anxiety. I imagine that you can associate these words on the page with a physical sensation. We often feel a moment of self-doubt in our body. It's the sensation of our body readying itself against a threat; the fight or flight response in action. I love the way that Paralympian Stef Reid talked about nerves on the High Performance podcast: 'Make friends with the butterflies... it's your body getting ready to go.'[12] This

---

[12] Humphries and Hughes, The High Performance Podcast Episode 174 – Stef Reid (23 January 2023).

is such a useful reminder. Your butterflies are not there as a warning or a signal that you're not up to the task. Your body is not trying to sabotage you. It's getting ready to go. There are a couple of simple things you can do when you notice your butterflies. The two practices described below can help you to settle, taking the body's stress meter down a notch. Neither of these exercises require any explanation to those around you; it's unlikely that anyone will notice what you're doing. You can quietly settle yourself, getting ready to do yourself justice.

COACH YOURSELF CONFIDENT #7

 PRACTICE: Settle yourself

Focus on your breathing

First, just notice... Are you breathing in through your nose or your mouth? Are you breathing shallowly into your chest or deeply into your diaphragm? You could count your in breaths and gradually try to slow down the rhythm.

If you need to further settle yourself, you could try a simple box breathing exercise, which signals to your body that you are safe:

1. Exhale to a count of four
2. Hold your lungs empty for a count of four
3. Inhale to a count of four
4. Hold the air in your lungs for a count of four
5. Exhale and begin the pattern anew

Physical touch

Our skin is an incredibly sensitive organ, and research indicates that physical touch releases oxytocin (which helps to regulate our emotional response), provides a sense of security, and calms cardiovascular stress.[13] So why not try it?

Depending on what you are wearing, you could find a way to lay a hand on your bare skin. In short sleeves, this could be by purposefully folding your arms and gently holding your upper arms with your hands. In long sleeves, you might try putting a hand to the back of your neck and holding it there for a moment while you gently move your head from side to side, or forward and back.

Counting the cost

As you continue to read this chapter, I invite you to notice what resonates. This is a way to quantify the self-doubt tax that you are currently paying. In the reflection activity below, I've set out the themes that we'll be exploring. A simple way to capture your thoughts is to create your own version of these two columns in your notebook. As you read through each section, you can note down your reflections and examples of how these themes play out for you.

---

[13] See https://self-compassion.org/exercise-4-supportive-touch/ (accessed 9 May 2023).

COACH YOURSELF CONFIDENT #8

 REFLECTION: Your self-doubt tax return

Missed opportunities	Overwork and exhaustion
Holding back	An achievement addiction
Staying small	
Slowing the pace	Hero complex
Leaving potential unfulfilled	Over preparation
	Emotional exhaustion

Paying the self-doubt tax in missed opportunities

Let's explore the first way that the self-doubt tax can be levied; missed opportunities and unfulfilled potential. Self-doubt can slow us down, and at its worst, self-doubt can keep us at a standstill. In the grip of self-doubt, we seek to keep ourselves safe by holding back. As Ian Robertson puts it in his book *How Confidence Works*: 'Fear means that you feel threatened, and when you feel unsafe, the only real alternatives are fight and flight… If the threat seems to come from inside you, there's nothing to fight. So flight becomes the only option, and the safe and familiar your only refuge.'[14]

---

[14] Robertson, 2021.

Sticking with the safe and familiar is understandable. It's comfortable and it can feel like the only sensible path, but it means that we miss out on opportunities, big and small. In the following sections, I'll bring to life what this version of the self-doubt tax looks like, drawing on what I've seen in my coaching work. The anonymized client stories that I share below are real, and I'm sharing them in the hope that they might illuminate your own experience.

Holding back

Sometimes silence is the way that self-doubt shows up; silence as a way of avoiding being noticed or avoiding the risk of an unfavourable response from others. It takes confidence to voice an opinion, and for some people it's incredibly difficult to push past the self-doubt and access the confidence that's needed to speak up.

My coaching client Oliver was frequently silent in meetings. Despite his experience and evident grasp of his specialism, he found it difficult to speak up and often missed the opportunity to be heard. As we explored Oliver's tendency to hold back, it became clear that he was staying quiet because of doubt that he could match up to the high standard that he'd set for himself. Irritated by colleagues who seemed to use a lot of words but not really say very much, Oliver adopted a rule that he would only speak up if his contribution was original, compelling and succinct. His high bar for contributions didn't allow him to build on someone else's point or refer back to something that came up previously. He gave himself no permission to start speaking and shape his thoughts as he heard them, and he allowed himself no room for the sort of statement of the obvious that can be incredibly useful in moving a conversation forward.

Oliver was only confident to speak when he was sure that all three of his internal criteria had been met, and given the exacting nature of those criteria, he was rarely confident enough to join the discussion. By censoring himself in this way, Oliver missed the opportunity to shape the thinking in the organization and missed the opportunity to allow colleagues to see the full extent of his capability.

It's not only the kind of exacting criteria that Oliver applied that stops individuals from speaking up. Self-doubt in the form of 'who am I to contribute?' can lead people to hold back. As part of my research, I had a fascinating conversation with a leader in the people function of a big UK retailer. As the person accountable for early careers, she is close to the graduates who join the business each year on an accelerated training programme. She reflected on a theme that she frequently sees amongst the company's graduate trainees, telling me: 'This kind of imposter syndrome plays out: "I'm just the grad, so nobody's going to want to listen to me." And that thought leads them to stay quiet. Staying quiet stops them from adding value in the meeting, and they start to feel like they don't have any value that they can bring.' Self-doubt leads them to stay quiet and staying quiet leads them to further doubt themselves.

Another way in which we might hold back is in suppressing what we think in order to please others. When our focus is on pleasing others, we miss the opportunity to fully be ourselves, saying what we think others want to hear rather than what we really think. This does not have to be a dramatic diversion from our own opinion, it can be a matter of emphasis, but nevertheless, even in this subtle way, we are editing what we say on the basis of how we think it will be received; we're not sharing our full thinking or our unique perspective. When fuelled by self-doubt, people pleasing is an attempt to avoid the risk of disappointing people. If we disappoint others, then they might think badly of us in some way; they might downgrade their evaluation of our capability. Framed in this way, disappointing others is simply too great a risk to take, so we might swallow disagreement or withhold controversial views, possibly storing up frustration and resentment. We find ourselves committed to a strategy that we do not believe in and then kick ourselves further down the line when our unvoiced fears become reality.

A few years back, I coached Fiona, a senior supply chain leader at a global organization. Fiona's version of pleasing others was putting on a mask when she stepped into the global executive forums at her organization. Feeling ill at ease at this level of seniority, Fiona observed her colleagues closely and identified what she saw as the accepted way of operating in the very top tier of the organization. This version of leadership didn't look like her own way of being a leader, so Fiona's assumption was that she must adapt. She thought that she had to act in the same way as her peers in order to be accepted and valued by them. In doing so, she was hiding herself, including all of the aspects of her leadership that had driven her success to that point. Not only was this exhausting, but it took away the opportunity for her peers and sponsors to see who Fiona really was, and to see what she stood for. Paradoxically, by seeking to mould herself to fit the template she perceived, she reduced the likelihood of being recognized as the talented, values-driven leader that she was. She presented a small and censored version of herself. She held back.

Is there anything to capture on your self-doubt tax return in the territory of 'holding back'?

Staying small

Seventeen years ago, I was co-facilitating a leadership programme at PepsiCo. The participants were impressive leaders from across the UK business who had been selected on the basis of their potential to reach the top of the organization. They were all one or two grades above my position in the organization and they were expected to progress quickly. On the last day of the programme, everyone was gathered in a large room in a circle of comfy chairs. Without conscious thought, I stationed myself on the outside of the circle. One of the participants, an inclusive and warm leader named Phil, got up and pulled my chair forward to bring me into the circle. The 2006 version of me did not feel comfortable to take up space in that room. It took Phil's invitation (insistence) for me to take my place within the circle. The events of those few minutes 17 years ago have remained vivid in my memory because it was a significant moment of realization for me: *I'm making myself small and I can choose to stop.*

I know, from my coaching and from the conversations that have shaped this book, that the temptation to be small is commonly experienced and difficult to resist. At its heart, it is an attempt to avoid visibility because with visibility comes the risk of judgement. Do you ever find yourself choosing to stay small in a discussion? Perhaps you don't believe that your thoughts warrant the same space as the ideas of those other (more capable) people in the room? Do you ever hear yourself speaking really quickly, as though you're keen to take up the least air space possible, getting your contribution out of the way quickly so that the other (better informed) participants can speak? These are both ways of taking up less verbal space.

Self-doubt can lead us to make ourselves physically small. In a bid not to be noticed, we shrink in our seat, or we fold in on ourselves with crossed arms, hunched posture, bowed heads. It's a way of hiding. In 2012, American social psychologist Amy Cuddy gave a TED talk called 'Your body language may shape who you are.' It's one of the most watched TED talks of all time, with over 68 million views. According to Cuddy, the way in which we carry our bodies affects how we feel about ourselves, how we interact with others, how we perform. In her talk, Cuddy talks about expansive and contractive postures. A contractive posture is the crossed arms and hunched over, bowed head. An expansive posture is one which sees us taking up more space; shoulders back, head up, feet planted firmly on the ground. We might even put our hands on our hips, elbows out, to take up more space. The expansive posture gives an impression of greater solidity and certainty.

Cuddy called this expansive stance a power pose and suggested that power posing – standing in a posture of confidence, even when we don't feel confident – can boost feelings of confidence. Since her 2012 talk, Cuddy has developed the idea further and says: 'It's not just about standing like a superhero for two minutes; it's about carrying yourself with power and pride and poise, as you deserve to do.'[15] The idea of power posing has not been without controversy, with arguments about whether our posture makes the significant difference claimed by Cuddy. A 2020 review of all the studies on posture showed that adopting an expansive stance – a power pose – doesn't raise confidence much at all. Importantly, however, the review also concluded that shrinking your posture – adopting a constrictive stance – diminished people's confidence quite significantly.[16]

COACH YOURSELF CONFIDENT #9

 PRACTICE: Take up space

Next time you notice that you are feeling nervous, try consciously rolling back your shoulders, lifting your chin and standing straight (or sitting tall in your chair).

Tune in to how you feel in that moment – does your posture help you to quieten your self-doubt and access your confidence?

---

[15] See https://ideas.ted.com/inside-the-debate-about-power-posing-a-q-a-with-amy-cuddy/ (accessed 9 May 2023).

[16] Robertson, 2021.

Another way of staying small is in our strategies, actions and plans. Here, staying small means erring on the side of caution, focusing on incremental improvements rather than radical change. It's a play-it-safe tactic that protects us from the risk of failing big, but it also 'protects' us from the possibility of succeeding big. I see clients play it safe with business plans and with career plans. I vividly remember my coaching client Jennifer wrestling with a stay-or-go decision. She wasn't enjoying her role and was feeling deeply unhappy but felt too uncertain of herself to leave. Her self-doubt kept her trapped. She felt so unsure of her ability to succeed elsewhere that she remained in a role that was making her unhappy, feeling in her own words 'like a hostage'.

Has anything about 'staying small' resonated with you? If so, add a note to your self-doubt tax return.

Slowing the pace

Procrastination is the enemy of pace and leads to missed opportunities. It can also come with a big helping of anxiety and guilt: *I know that this needs doing, I'm putting it off, my manager will be chasing, I really should be getting this done.* Self-doubt triggered procrastination comes in a few different flavours:

- *I don't even know where to start* – just thinking about the task evokes a mild sense of panic. It's impossible to access our rational thinking and problem solving capabilities because they are hidden behind the big blocker in our minds: *I cannot do this! I cannot do this!*

- *I can't get it wrong* – we can't bear the idea of failure and we postpone the possibility of failure by not getting started. We can't fail if we don't do it at all.
- *It must be perfect* – we set ourselves an intimidatingly high standard which (unsurprisingly) feels impossible. We're not quite ready to deliver perfection, so we'll just do something else before we start, perhaps a little more research will help me to do a better job?

Procrastination is one of those self-defeating habits that is simultaneously really frustrating and hard to kick. My coaching client Billy knew his pattern well: 'One of the things that stops me quite often is a view that my current thinking is not yet 100%. It stops me from getting started.' His procrastination was of the 'it must be perfect' variety, and the remedy that he found was to ensure that inaction was not an option. When Billy noticed that he was treading water on developing his new strategy, he scheduled a meeting with his boss with the stated objective of talking through the strategy document. The intention was to make doing the work unavoidable because the discomfort associated with turning up to that meeting without a strategy was greater than the discomfort of putting fingers to keyboard before he'd worked everything out in his head.

Please take a moment now to reflect on your own experience of procrastination and add notes to your self-doubt tax return if need be.

Leaving potential unfulfilled

All too often, the combined impact of holding back, staying small and slowing the pace is unfulfilled potential.

We underestimate ourselves, holding back from career opportunities, and our self-doubt leads others to underestimate us too. Unfulfilled potential is a particularly painful way in which the self-doubt tax is paid; not reaching (or perhaps not even seeing) the boundaries of your capacity to grow. You pay that tax in satisfaction, and perhaps even in unearned salary. And your organization misses out too; it misses out on the full extent of the contribution that you could make if self-doubt wasn't holding you back.

Sometimes there's a part of us that knows how good we are. But it's a part of us that is fragile, a part of us that we don't listen to very often. It speaks up when we see a colleague celebrating their promotion to a role that we have the skills to do. It stayed quiet when we saw the advert for that role, so we didn't apply. We'll explore this further when we look at faulty calibration in Chapter 4. For now, I just want to note how much it can hurt when we know that we are capable of more, but that we are holding ourselves back. It can feel like we're stuck in a double bind: *If I don't go for a role, I won't be rejected. But I also won't be accepted.*

Daniel, a participant on one of my leadership programmes, nearly missed out on the high profile, high impact job that he now enjoys. He was fortunate enough to have a boss who saved him from himself. 'Caroline saw something in me. She pushed me. What an amazing opportunity that I nearly threw away due to my lack of confidence.' Daniel is not alone; there are many self-doubters whose payment of the self-doubt tax has been reduced due to the support, sponsorship and (well intentioned) shoving of colleagues who had a clear-sighted view of their potential. In Chapter 7, we'll look at the impact of supporters, and how absorbing and internalizing their positive view of us can contribute to a robust sense of confidence.

Paying the self-doubt tax in overwork

It's perfectly possible to be under-confident and wildly successful, but there's a cost. 'I have this irrational fear that I'm going to get fired. I know it's irrational, but it's still there – I can't get rid of it.' Orlagh moved between laughter and exasperation as she explored her hidden fear with me during a coaching session. She could see that her fear was without basis as she could find no evidence to suggest a likelihood that she was about to be fired. And yet those rational thoughts were not enough to counter the fear; she simply couldn't shake it off. Seen by others as sparky, dynamic and brilliant, Orlagh expended significant energy in *both* battling her inner critic *and* hiding that battle from colleagues. It was only at home or within the safety of a coaching relationship that she was able to give voice to her fear. Orlagh was (and still is) hugely successful in her career, *and* she was weighed down by an inner commentary of doubt – a commentary that led her to work punishing hours. Orlagh's self-doubt tax was payable in the currency of overwork and exhaustion.

I've met and worked with many people like Orlagh. Incredibly successful individuals whose success has partly been driven by their self-doubt. In order to lessen their anxiety, they have pushed themselves excessively hard. Let's take a closer look at this form of the self-doubt tax.

Achievement addiction

In Greek mythology, the gods punish Sisyphus for his arrogance by sentencing him to push a huge boulder uphill for all eternity. It's a never-ending task because every time Sisyphus reaches the top of the hill, the boulder rolls back down again. He's condemned to interminable hard labour. For some self-doubt taxpayers, their exhaustion stems from their own, self-imposed Sisyphean task from which there seems to be no respite. Their interminable hard labour is in the form of constantly achieving, and it means that they do more and more and more. It's exhausting.

In place of a well of inner confidence that's based on an appreciation of their own capabilities, these self-doubt taxpayers have a bucket of achievement. It's their bucket of achievement that reassures them that they are worthy, that they should be in this job, that they're not an imposter. The achievements are essential to obscure their self-doubt from themselves and to obscure what they see as their weaknesses or inadequacies from others. The problem is that the bucket has a hole in it, meaning that it has to be continuously topped up. The individual cannot enjoy their achievements because they must always look for the next one; they must always do more. These individuals are on the treadmill of hard work, chasing achievement in order to shore up their belief in themselves.

My coaching client Zara consistently worked six or seven days a week, often until the early hours of the morning on weeknights. Concerned about her, Zara's husband would encourage her to close the laptop and would sometimes get frustrated when she did not. Zara told me of a Saturday afternoon when she put on her sports kit and told her husband that she was going to the gym. She smuggled her laptop out in her gym bag, drove to the gym car park, then sat in her car and caught up on emails. She even went as far as doing a sprint round the block before returning home to ensure that she'd look convincingly red and sweaty. She could see that this was unusual behaviour, but she could not allow herself a different choice. In her mind, the work just had to be done.

Zara loved her job, but there was more to her excessively hard work. Having made it to a director role, she gripped tightly to it, fearful that she might be 'found out' if she didn't dedicate herself to it entirely. Everything that she had already achieved for the organization somehow no longer counted and she felt a compulsion to deliver more and more. By a number of measures, Zara had already transformed the performance of her part of the business and yet still thought 'I need to start making a difference. I need to work my arse off this year.' Zara only knew that she could do the job by proving it to herself, and that process was never ending. She put herself through a continuous process of evaluation – she was only ever in a trial period, her position insecure.

Zara is far from alone. I remember my coaching client Arjun, who talked eloquently about feeling unable to take his foot off the accelerator. He never felt that he had delivered enough because in his mind the list of 'should haves' loomed large. He based his confidence on what he had delivered – his 'have done' list was the way that he proved to himself that he was doing a good job. But despite this, he placed more emphasis on those opportunities not yet taken. Like Zara, Arjun struggled to calibrate a realistic expectation of achievement, based not only on the capacity of himself and his team, but also on the context in which he was operating. We'll look at Arjun's story again in Chapter 4 when we explore faulty calibration.

During the research for this book, I came across an academic paper with what I thought to be a brilliantly clever name. 'Goal missed, self hit'[17] is the title that makes a powerful point within its sparse four words. The paper explores the psychological impacts of setting stretching goals with the finding that confidence levels are damaged when individuals set – and then fail to achieve – ambitious goals. 'Goal missed, self hit' is another way of articulating an element of the self-doubt tax. Zara and Arjun would be particularly vulnerable to this self injury because both of them combine a tendency to measure their own success by achievement with the setting of an unreasonably high bar. This combination of factors is a common one; they come together because they are overlapping, reinforcing. If I measure myself by what I achieve, keeping my confidence topped up by a continuous stream of achievements to which I can point, then I am driven to set ever more stretching targets. Like any other addiction, a stronger hit is needed as time goes by.

Is there anything about the 'achievement addiction' that feels familiar to you? What might you need to note down on your self-doubt tax return?

---

[17] Höpfner and Keith, 2021.

Hero complex

At first sight, this seems paradoxical: self-doubters who have a hero complex. How can someone lack confidence and yet see themselves as the only person who can save the day? The answer lies in what sits behind the hero complex. For the self-doubt taxpayer, heroism stems not from ego (*I'm exceptionally talented*) but from an intense need to prove (*Look - I am good enough after all!*). This need to prove is as much about demonstrating their capabilities to themselves as it is about proving themselves to others.

In the early days of my coaching relationship with Chloe, a senior executive in consumer packaged goods, she was grappling with a number of big, gnarly, systemic issues. She appeared to be on a one-person crusade to challenge what she saw as faulty thinking at the top of the organization and to push for significant change. Chloe's manager advised her to reach out to others, to form a coalition, but Chloe resisted. 'I consider myself capable and I don't want to be constantly knocking on doors.' She was seeing collaboration as a sign of not being good enough, believing that she should be able to deal with it on her own. The irony was that Chloe's hero complex – the intense need to show that she alone could fix things – took her away from her shining strength. A natural relationship builder, Chloe collaborates easily and has built a web of meaningful connections across a complex global organization. Exhausted, under pressure and her confidence at a low ebb, Chloe couldn't see that her power would stem from her ability to build a coalition for change. Once she was able to set down the heavy weight of solo responsibility that she had placed on her own shoulders, she began to engage with others and created meaningful change.

Is there anything to add to your self-doubt tax return? Do you recognize anything of this heroic need to prove?

Over preparation

I have a self-doubt habit that stays with me. Over preparation is a habit that I can't fully kick despite an increase in confidence through the years. For me, over preparing is a way of calming the fear of not meeting my own high standards or not being seen as brilliant at what I do. My over preparation is the investment of more time and energy than is necessary, going beyond the sort of professionalism and focus that my clients have every right to expect of me. I continue to tweak a workshop design that is already fit for purpose. I go beyond a simple plan for an upcoming conversation and begin to rehearse what I might say. My over preparation is not only the kind of active work that's done at my desk, but it can also be a less focused, distracting kind of preparation that happens in swirls inside my head as I approach a session that I anticipate might be tricky.

The over preparation habit is (unfortunately) a common one, and it's one of the contributors to the additional hours that can lead to the self-doubt tax of exhaustion. It's both reassuring and depressing that I share this habit with many people, including individuals who are incredibly successful in their field. In her memoir, *Airhead*, British journalist and broadcaster Emily Maitlis told the story of chairing a live TV debate between the five candidates vying to replace Theresa May as Conservative Party Leader and Prime Minister of the UK. It was a high profile assignment and not surprisingly involved a really long working day with Maitlis leaving the studio close to midnight.

Having agreed to appear on live radio the following morning to analyse the performance of the debate contenders, Maitlis set an alarm for 8.30am, which would give her 20 minutes before she was due to be live on air. As she describes, this plan to allow herself a good amount of rest went awry. '"I'll wing it," I think. But my subconscious knows better. I wake, as I should have predicted I would, at 4am. Winging it is for the men, perhaps. I cannot do insouciance as readily as I pretend I can. I need my notes. My collected thoughts. My felt-tip highlighter pens.' Even though her rational brain knew that she could go straight into the live interview, Maitlis's subconscious wouldn't allow her to do so. Her subconscious insisted on a few hours of preparation for something that she was already prepared to do. This kind of over preparation adds up. Workload is inflated and working hours are extended by preparation, which is necessary only because it is a substitute for self-trust.

If you recognize yourself as an over preparer, as well as making a note on your self-doubt tax return, I invite you to have a go at the activity below.

COACH YOURSELF CONFIDENT #10

 PRACTICE: Preparation calibration

Choose an upcoming meeting, something that will require some preparation.

1. Write a sentence or two to define the desired outcome of the meeting from your perspective.

2. If you were to go into the meeting right now, in what ways would you be equipped to achieve that outcome? (What do you already know? What experience do you carry with you? What preparation have you already done? How has preparation for other interactions informed your thinking?)

3. What's the fullest version of preparation that you could choose to do? Indulge your instinct to over-prepare – what would over preparation look like in this case? Write it all down.

4. Now take a red pen (metaphorically or literally) to the list that you created at step 3. In the spirit of right-sizing your preparation, what will you cross off and what will you choose to do?

5. Finally, reflect on your experience of doing this exercise: What has come up for you in relation to a habit of over preparation? What will you note down on your self-doubt tax return? Is there anything from this exercise that you will carry forward into your day-to-day ways of working?

Emotional exhaustion

A coaching client, Sophie, was recently promoted to the executive team of her organization. Stepping into a C-suite role was a long-held aspiration for Sophie and something that she had worked hard to achieve. On the day that she was told the job was hers, Sophie experienced a dizzying array of emotions. Her bright smile faded as she walked out of the CEO's office and out to the car park. Reaching for her phone, Sophie texted her sister: 'I got it! What?! I feel sick!!' A few moments later, Sophie sent a second message to her sister: 'What on earth made me think I could do this?!' Although a part of Sophie could see that she had the capabilities and experience to operate as the Chief Financial Officer, another part of her held tight to self-doubt. Going for the role had involved squashing the doubting part of her, and at the very moment of her success that doubt rebounded with a fervour. As Sophie was congratulated by colleagues in the days following her appointment, she found herself on an exhausting emotional rollercoaster. On an hourly basis, she pinged between feeling excited and proud, and feeling inadequate and terrified.

Alongside the mental effort required to shape her approach to the new role and begin to lead the function, Sophie expended significant energy in managing her emotional state. As someone who has long paid the self-doubt tax in the form of overwork, this emotional stress added to an existing level of exhaustion.

Is there anything about the idea of emotional exhaustion that resonates with you? You might want to take a moment to add a note or two to your self-doubt tax return.

Show yourself some compassion

As we approach the end of this chapter on the self-doubt tax, I hope you are deepening your awareness of the level of self-doubt tax that you are paying. I hope also that the preceding pages have offered you some ideas about ways in which you could reduce your self-doubt tax payment. To close this chapter, I'm inviting you to consider how you might be a little kinder to yourself. Let's start with an imaginary conversation in the run up to an executive board meeting at which your colleague is requesting sign-off for a significant project.

Your colleague: I'm not looking forward to the exec meeting at all. My stomach is churning.

You: You should be nervous! You're pretty hopeless at getting your point across, aren't you? I find it hard to believe that your boss is letting you do this, to be honest. They must know you'll balls it up. Can you just pretend to be ill and get someone else to do it?

Do you recognize yourself in this script? Of course you don't (or I certainly hope not). This imaginary version of you is brutal with your colleague. It's much more likely that you would respond with compassion. Offering yourself compassion is another way to lessen the power of your inner critic and to access your confidence.

I imagine that you'll be familiar with what's known as the golden rule: 'Treat others as you would like to be treated.' A choice to show yourself some compassion means that you apply a version of this golden rule to yourself – that you treat yourself as you would treat others. It means extending to yourself the kindness of a friend who wants to help you to learn and grow, a friend who is willing to offer a useful and objective evaluation of your performance as a counter to the harsh judgement of your inner critic. For example, 'I completely messed that up, I'm a terrible facilitator' becomes 'That wasn't my finest hour, there are learnings for next time.'

COACH YOURSELF CONFIDENT #11

 PRACTICE: Treat yourself as you would treat others

This is an in-the-moment tool that you can use when you notice that you are being hard on yourself, allowing your inner critic to step into the spotlight. It's a way of accessing self-compassion.

1. Pause and take a breath.

2. Ask yourself: If a friend were to find themselves in the situation that I'm in right now, what would I say to them?

To sum up...

- When our self-doubt is over-sized, a self-doubt tax payment becomes due.

- Although well intentioned, our inner critic can be a loud and diminishing presence. We can lessen their impact by keeping our distance – evaluating what they tell us rather than accepting their words as fact.

- The language that we use impacts how we feel about ourselves as well as how others see us. Our choice of words can diminish or build confidence in our own eyes and in the eyes of those around us.

- When we allow a lack of confidence to hold us back, we play small and play safe, paying the self-doubt tax in the form of missed opportunities and unfulfilled potential.

- When we push ourselves to achieve impressive results despite a nagging self-doubt, we pay the tax in the form of overwork and exhaustion, with self-defeating habits such as an addiction to achievement, over preparation and punishingly high standards.

- By closing the gap between our actual capability and our confidence (what we believe ourselves to be capable of), we can right-size our self-doubt and lower our self-doubt tax burden.

3

The humble confidence benefit

When it comes to confidence, more is not always better. Our aim is not to build our confidence level ever higher, our aim is to build just the right amount. The Goldilocks approach to confidence. 'Just the right amount' is a level of confidence that matches our capability. With just the right amount of confidence, our sense of what we are capable of aligns with the reality of our skills and abilities. We don't inflate our sense of self with grandiose opinions about what we bring and an exaggeration of our abilities. Neither do we allow excessive self-doubt to diminish our understanding of who we are and what we bring. We experience human self-doubt, but not to the degree that a self-doubt tax payment becomes due.

I call this balanced and objective sense of self 'humble confidence', and it's the type of self-belief that *Coach Yourself Confident* will support you to develop. With humble confidence, we are able to take a clear-sighted look at our strengths, our achievements and our opportunities to develop. Humble confidence isn't static. 'Just the right amount' of confidence is the level that matches our skills and abilities, so as we expand our capability we expand our confidence. In this chapter, we'll explore humble confidence, and we'll unpack the humble confidence mantra: I am good enough *and* I can be better.

Painting a picture

To begin our exploration of humble confidence, let's look at the origin of the word 'humble'. The word 'humility' derives from the Latin *humus*, meaning 'earth'. Humble confidence is grounded confidence; grounded in reality and grounded in an objective perspective of our capability. If we're humble, we have the ability to accurately assess our success and we can be OK with our inevitable, ordinary, human limitations. This is what humble confidence sounds like:

- My strengths are clear to me. I know what I'm good at.
- I know what I'm not so good at, and I'm OK with that.

- I know that I can add to my list of strengths through focus and effort.
- I have navigated some tricky situations and I've come out the other side.
- If need be, I can navigate adversity again.
- I can face the unknown with a sense that I'll find what's needed within myself.

Humble confidence is a solid and balanced sense of self, neither inflating egotism nor diminishing self-doubt. The sentences arc founded on 'I' – they are about my own knowledge of myself, rather than relying on how others see me. These are not mantras to recite, they are articulations of a felt experience. I am not seeking to convince anyone – either myself or others – of my abilities or my self-assurance, I'm simply noticing what is true for me. It's a sense of self that can endure and that is portable from context to context.

Let's look at humble confidence in action. When Uma Rajah, the co-founder and CEO of online property investment firm CapitalRise, told me her story, what stood out to me was her capacity to see her own capabilities (and the external context) in a clear and realistic way. Towards the end of 2015, Uma was weighing up three job offers. Two of the offers would have been a natural extension of Uma's CV to date, building on her proven track record. 'I felt very confident about those ones – I'd been there, done that, got the T-shirt.' The third offer was something different. Alex Michelin, the person behind the idea for CapitalRise, asked Uma to co-found the business with him and his business partner, Andrew Dunn. Uma would be employee number one, with responsibility for establishing and growing CapitalRise and making Alex's idea a reality.

Having never before had sole responsibility at the very top of an organization, Uma took time to weigh up whether she could do the role, and whether she wanted to take on this level of challenge. There would be financial risk, 'an intense amount of work' and the uncertainty that comes with starting something new. As Uma pointed out to me: 'Unfortunately, the stats show that the majority of new businesses will fail, so the odds are stacked against you.'

In considering her own candidacy for the CEO job, there were multiple questions that Uma asked herself. Do I have the reserves to take on a start-up? (She knew first-hand that it could be a brutal experience, having co-founded a business in 2007 that did not survive the global financial crisis.) Do I have a sufficient financial safety net? Do I have the skills that are needed to make it a success? On the question of skills, Uma framed it as a question about the founding trio: rather than 'Do I individually have all of the skills?' she asked, 'Do we collectively have the skills required?' Applying a clear-sighted rigour to this question, Uma could see that she personally brought something critical, and that the combination of skills and experience within the founding trio meant that collectively they had the requisite capabilities. 'I had no concerns about the part of the job that Andrew and Alex absolutely needed me to do. They had never built a technology platform like the one that we've built, and I had built nine by the time I took this job. They had already built a successful business, so even if I was really terrible at the parts that I'd never done before, they were tried and tested real estate entrepreneurs and I could learn from them. There was a safety net for the specific areas where I didn't have any prior experience.'

Uma had the confidence to back herself, clearly seeing the value that she would add. She also had the humility to recognize that there would be a learning process as she stepped into the CEO role. This wasn't a case of being wracked by self-doubt, but a clarity on the elements of the role that would be new to her. She didn't shy away from the opportunity and neither did she feel a need to bluff her way through and try to prove that she could do it. She accepted her strengths and her gaps, and welcomed the support from her co-founders as she grew into the role.

Uma modelled an openness to collaboration and a welcoming of support that forms a core element of humble confidence. Leadership is not a lone venture, even for solo entrepreneurs. Humble confidence says *I don't need to be the expert in everything*. Instead, the critical capability is to identify what's needed, and then to evaluate (without ego) what you can do and where you need help. It's easier to seek out help if you have humble confidence because you don't feel the compulsion to prove. You know that you're good enough, and you're fully aware of your gaps. You're comfortable with the truth that there will always be more that you can learn. We'll dig into this truth as we explore the humble confidence mantra.

The humble confidence mantra

With humble confidence, we can own our strengths. We can straightforwardly say 'I'm a strong strategist' or 'I connect well with people; I build trusting relationships.' We know what we're good at. When someone talks positively about our capabilities, we can accept their praise because we see those capabilities too. And yet at the same time, we know that there will always be ways that we can grow and develop, that it's always possible to add more strengths to our repertoire, that as human beings we're never going to be the finished article. *I am good enough and I can be better* is the mantra of humble confidence.

This mantra underpins confidence without complacency in our areas of expertise and it underpins confidence in new areas. We can be confident even when we're a novice at something because our self-belief isn't tied up in our ability to do this new thing (we are already good enough, even without this skill) and because we know that we can learn. We can have a realistic expectation of our own capability in a new skill (or a new role, a new context), and we can back ourselves to develop fast because we can learn. We can get better.

There are two parts to the humble confidence mantra, both of which are important, so I'll unpack each element of the phrase in turn. *I am good enough* is settling and affirming. It's a belief that allows us to let go of any need to prove and any inclination to berate ourselves about what we lack. In the words of coach and author, Becky Hall: 'When we believe that we are enough, we can find freedom and flow that allows us to shine.'[18] I invite you to complete the reflection activity below, focusing on the *I am good enough* part of our humble confidence mantra.

---

[18] Hall, 2021.

COACH YOURSELF CONFIDENT #12

 REFLECTION: I am good enough

Step 1

Grab a piece of paper and write the sentence starter 'When I am at my best, I...' at the top.

Now set a timer for five minutes.

In that five minutes, write down as many versions as you can come up with for what comes after that sentence starter. What you're doing here is writing about your strengths in action, e.g. 'When I'm at my best, I can inspire my team by setting out a clear and ambitious vision.'

Step 2

Now have a read of your list and consider these questions:

- What was it like to write the list of your strengths?
- What was it like to read your list of strengths?
- Are there any more strengths to add?

Now let's look at the second part of our mantra: *and I can be better*. These five words represent a forward-looking belief in better that comes not from a place of self-doubt, but from a commitment to growth. A quest to improve that's fuelled by a thirst for learning rather than a compulsion to compensate for something that we lack. There is no lack: we are already good enough.

And I can be better allows us to see the gap between the current and the possible through a lens of curiosity – what can we learn? What's our next step forward? In this way, the gap represents opportunity. When I spoke to Olympic gold medallist Kate Richardson-Walsh, one of the themes that shone through was the essence of the humble confidence mantra: self-belief combined with a commitment to improve. In Kate's words, 'a constant thought from when I got into the senior Great Britain hockey team at 19, all the way to the end of my playing career at the age of 36 was *I can always do this better*. Even after the Olympic final in which we won gold, even after I retired, I was still thinking *if I had my time again, I would do this instead of that*.'

There's an inbuilt optimism in the words *I can be better*, an optimism that encourages you to put in the time and practice that's needed in order to develop. This second part of our mantra embodies what psychology Professor Carol Dweck terms a 'growth mindset'; the belief that we can grow, learn and change for the better, through failure and success alike. A growth mindset motivates us to try, to reflect, to get back up after a setback, to ask for help, to learn because we believe that doing these things will unlock growth. We're not limited to a set of talents that we were born with but can develop skill in (almost) anything if we apply focus and commitment. We can be better.

Before we get carried away with growth mindset, let's be clear that the constraints of reality do still apply. Adopting a growth mindset doesn't mean that with the proper motivation, training and practice, any of us could become an Olympic rower, a famous musician or an astrophysicist. There are other things at play, for example, an Olympic rower probably has some physical advantages bestowed on them by genetics. Having a growth mindset doesn't mean that anyone can do absolutely anything at the highest level. Rather, the principle behind growth mindset is that a person's potential is unknowable; it's impossible to foresee what could be accomplished with commitment, passion, toil and training. Neuroscience offers some evidence for this idea, outlined here in the words of Michael Merzenich: 'The brain is designed to change. You are designed to be continuously improvable. Nobody's done. Nobody's defined what their limits are. I can tell you, whatever you think your limits are, you're wrong. Absolutely everyone has the capacity to be better at virtually everything.'[19] There's science behind the humble confidence mantra! There's no limit to *better*.

The last exercise was focused on the *I am good enough* part of our humble confidence mantra. For the next one, I invite you to consider the second part: *and I can be better*.

COACH YOURSELF CONFIDENT #13

 REFLECTION: And I can be better

Step 1

The process for this exercise is the same as the last one (#12). There's a sentence starter and you give yourself five minutes to complete the sentence in as many ways as you can.

---

[19] Merzenich, 2013.

The sentence starter this time is: 'To make my contribution *even better*, I would like to...' e.g. 'To make my contribution even better, I would like to find ways to spend more time on strategy and less time on running the day-to-day.'

Step 2

Read through your list.

- How does it compare to the list that you wrote in the *I am good enough* exercise? (#12)
- Is it shorter or longer?
- Was it easier or harder to write?
- How does it feel as you read it back?

Step 3

Take a few minutes to look back over everything that you have written down for this exercise and the *I am good enough* exercise (#12).

Now say (or write down) the humble confidence mantra: *I am good enough and I can be better.* How does that mantra fit for you? Is it something that you can apply to yourself?

If it doesn't yet feel comfortable, make some notes on what it is about the mantra that makes it difficult for you to accept – this is useful data as you continue to coach yourself confident.

We can apply a version of the humble confidence mantra to the results that we deliver: what I've done is good enough *and* there's always room to improve. We take satisfaction from our achievements and feel proud of what we have accomplished. And at the same time, we are clear that more is possible. *I've done a brilliant job this year and there are more opportunities to go after in the next 12 months. I'm delighted that I've achieved the goal that I set for myself and I'm thinking about what's next.* It's enough. And more is possible. This way of thinking can be an antidote to the compulsion to work harder and harder that showed up as a form of the self-doubt tax. I recognize that it can be tricky to identify what constitutes 'enough'; we'll explore this in some depth in the next chapter.

Right-sized self-doubt

Developing humble confidence enables us to stop paying the self-doubt tax, but it does not mean eradicating self-doubt. Humble confidence cuts our self-doubt down to size, sloughing off the excess upon which the tax is levied. In Uma Rajah's contemplation of the CEO role, her doubts were right-sized, stemming from a clear-sighted assessment of how her experience to date prepared her to do the job. Uma's doubts – neither unwarranted nor inflated – helped her to inform her decision to take the role. This is an example of right-sized self-doubt enabling right-sized response. With this right-sizing, the doubt that we feel informs how we move forward rather than preventing us from acting. We notice our doubt, think about what it might tell us, and take action anyway. We neither avoid the opportunity nor exhaust ourselves with excessive effort; we don't pay the self-doubt tax.

Right-sized self-doubt brings other benefits too. It fuels collaboration because we see where we excel *and* we see where we need help. We can get clear on the support that we need and seek out partners to collaborate with. Right-sized doubt enables right-sized preparation. We can prepare for an upcoming task and stop when we've done enough. We don't get caught in a trap of thinking that the more we do, the readier we will be. We can think ahead without catastrophizing. Right-sized doubt fuels open-mindedness and the ability to rethink. We can hold a point of view lightly, remaining open to new learning and acknowledging the possibility that our thinking is wrong. This light hold is not because we're wracked by self-doubt, but because we're fully aware of the limitations of human thinking and of the complexity of the world around us.

And arguably the biggest benefit of right-sized self-doubt is that it fuels curiosity and growth by prompting us to reflect on our approach in a bid to do even better next time. This is not the mental treadmill of overthinking but a productive process of reflection. Miranda Mapleton, CEO of the charity White Swan, describes it like this: 'Sometimes I think "I wish I'd handled that situation differently." I think everyone has those moments. What makes the difference is whether you think to yourself "I messed up, but it's OK because everyone needs to learn and do things differently", or you beat yourself up about it, telling yourself that you're a terrible leader because you handled that one situation wrongly.' The most constructive takeaway, the version that represents right-sized self-doubt, is *I'll do it differently next time*.

Getting too big for your boots

We're going to take a brief diversion into the territory of overconfidence where self-doubt is under-sized. I imagine that you've come across people whose mismatch between capability and confidence is the opposite to your own – their confidence outstrips their capability, meaning that rather than having 'just the right amount' of confidence, they have an excess. Or rather, I should say that they *appear* to have an excess because in my experience overconfidence is sometimes a front for insecurity. But that's a whole other book! For now, my reason for taking this brief diversion into overconfidence is to recognize that you might have some reservations about growing your confidence that stem from a fear of getting too big for your boots. As a side note, variations of this British idiom are also available. In Norway, rather than 'he's too big for his boots', the saying is 'Høy på pæren' that translates as 'he's high on the pear',[20] which I rather like! Anyway, let's venture into the territory of too much confidence for a short while, and then I'll tell you why I think that any fear of you getting too big for your boots is unfounded.

In the UK in the early 2000s, comedian Catherine Tate's television show included a series of sketches in which Catherine stepped in at the last moment to help someone out, with the reassuring phrase 'I can do that.' The comedy lay in the character's delusion. She confidently stepped in as a

---

[20] Groskop, 2023.

tennis player, salsa dancer, drummer and interpreter, doing a spectacularly bad job in every case. We've all come across this kind of delusion outside of TV comedies. I remember a fellow pupil in my A-level French class who was asked to translate part of our set text, Guy de Maupassant's *Boule de Suif*. She proceeded to confidently, and completely incorrectly, voice the English translation. It was as though she thought that conviction would be sufficient to make up for the inaccuracy; if I say it with confidence, no one will correct me, not even the teacher. I was impressed by her audacity and appalled by her imprecision in roughly equal measure.

Psychologists would call my classmate a bullshitter: someone who seeks to give an exaggerated impression of their knowledge.[21] Studies into the phenomenon of bullshitting make for entertaining reading. In one example, a proportion of the teenage participants asserted that they were completely familiar with the mathematical terms 'declarative fraction', 'subjunctive scaling' and 'proper number'. Their certainty was interesting given that these terms had been made up by the researchers; the concepts do not exist. Like Catherine Tate's 'I can do that' character, the teenagers who ticked the box to say that they knew all about declarative fractions were deluded. Their confidence exceeded their capability. Whilst the bullshitting studies are amusing, in a work setting, this kind of overconfidence can have serious negative consequences.

With an exaggerated evaluation of their capability and knowledge, it's easy for an overconfident person to fall into a trap of certainty and invincibility that distances them from

---

[21] Jerrim, Parker and Shure, 2019 cited in Robertson, 2021.

others. They are convinced that their ideas are the best ones, that their answer is the right one, that they know the way forward, so they have no need to listen to anyone else. They won't ask for input and they won't take on board feedback. They are dangerously self-sufficient. Nobody can see a situation from all possible angles, nobody can look at an issue through a lens that isn't tinged with their own (singular and therefore limited) life experience. The tunnel vision that comes with only taking notice of their own thinking leaves them open to making mistakes, to unknowingly taking risks, to delivering suboptimal performance.

A sense of caution against the possibility of overconfidence is understandable; overconfidence brings with it some significant risks. But I think that in your case such caution is unwarranted. We can imagine confidence as a continuum, with excess self-doubt (and under-sized confidence) at one end, and under-sized self-doubt (and excess confidence) at the other. It's not a case of either being at one end or the other, there's a big swathe of territory in between. If your start point is towards one end, then it's highly unlikely that you will swing all the way to the other end. Working on your excess self-doubt will not make you conceited. I come back to our aim: we're working to develop humble confidence, a 'just the right amount' level of confidence that aligns with your capability.

Uniquely you

Humble confidence is quiet, with no need to shout and no need to prove. There's an assurance that comes from the alignment of your confidence with your capability that allows you to be comfortable with being yourself. When you're weighed down by self-doubt, it can be easy to fall into the trap of trying to play the part of someone who is more confident, more capable, more worthy of being heard. With humble confidence, you are comfortable in your own skin, heeding the words of Maya Angelou: 'You alone are enough – you have nothing to prove to anybody.'

There's a 'comfortable in your own skin' thread that's woven through this book. It underpins the reflection exercises, all of which are founded on the idea that you already have what you need within you and that you just need a little support to fully access your confidence. Coaching yourself confident is fundamentally a process of finding *your* confidence. It's not about looking for confident people to emulate because there isn't a single version of confidence – it's much more personal than that. It's not about faking confidence in the hope that you can fool others, and ultimately fool yourself into greater confidence. It's about growing your confidence from within.

In doing the two exercises that I've offered so far in this chapter, you've been looking within. You've looked within at the strengths that you bring and at the opportunities that you see to 'be better'. In the final exercise in our chapter on the humble confidence benefit, we're turning our attention to another important element of your inner workings: your values. If we're clear on what's important to us, then we can act each day in ways that align with the values that we hold close. This congruence between our values and our actions can feed our confidence. We can feel more certain about a tricky decision if we've tested it against the gauge of our values. We can be more willing to voice an opinion that might be unpopular if we know that we're speaking from the heart.

COACH YOURSELF CONFIDENT #14

 REFLECTION: What matters most to me

The intention of this exercise is for you to identify (or reconfirm) what matters most to you. The aim is to end up with a handful of values that articulate what drives you and encapsulate how you want to be in the world.

I'm offering a range of values below, which I've categorized into six broad themes.

Take a bit of time now to highlight the values words that resonate most strongly for you. There is no right or wrong here – your values form part of 'unique you' so it's about capturing what's true for you, as opposed to listening to any sense of what 'should' be important to you.

You might need to do a few rounds of the exercise in order to whittle your list of values down to just a handful. I'd suggest that you're aiming for something in the region of five to seven values. You're not limited to the words that are here – if there's an important value that's missing, add it for yourself.

Once you've done this, make a diary note to come back to your list in a few days' time, to try it on for size and see if it still feels right to you.

Heart	Growth	Connection
Fairness	Challenge	Belonging
Honesty	Self-acceptance	Teamwork
Tolerance	Courage	Helping
Generosity	Adventure	Relationship
Integrity	Creativity	Respect
Forgiveness	Personal growth	Trust
Freedom	Perseverance	Consensus
Commitment	Resilience	Harmony
Altruism	Learning	Community

Structure	Accomplishment	Well-being
Tradition	Competence	Health
Security	Achievement	Pleasure
Stability	Knowledge	Play
Neatness	Recognition	Prosperity
Self-control	Authority	Family
Rationality	Power	Appearance
Rigour	Competition	Tenderness
Organization	Impact	Hedonism
Compliance	Advancement	Energy

A paradox

I want to end this chapter by recognizing a paradox. I have set out the case for humble confidence, and I believe that this well-calibrated, grounded sense of self is powerful. It enables action, curiosity and growth. A robust, internally generated feeling of humble confidence is a feeling that I'd like you to develop and nurture, and I'm hopeful that this process has already begun as you have gained insight from the stories and reflection exercises offered within this chapter. As you continue to read the book, my wish for you is that you become more intimately acquainted with your confidence and that you begin to better calibrate your strengths, weaknesses and contribution.

And yet, as you deepen your inquiry, as you coach yourself confident, I urge you to avoid falling into the trap of setting up humble confidence as a new bar to reach. If the idea of humble confidence becomes some kind of ideal that you now have to aspire to, then it becomes part of the problem. You set the bar out of reach and risk falling into a (perhaps familiar) pattern of focusing on the gap, berating yourself. If you don't achieve what you set out to do, you don't reach this new ideal, then you're not good enough. That's the paradox. I urge you to hold the aspiration to grow humble confidence lightly, to see it as an ongoing process rather than a task to achieve. Growing humble confidence isn't easy. I don't say this to discourage you. I say this to be realistic. If it were easy, then you wouldn't have picked up a copy of this book. Indeed, I wouldn't have written it. There would have been no need for it. Have faith in your capacity to grow your confidence and try to notice and appreciate all of the steps you take along the way, however small.

To sum up...

- With humble confidence, our sense of what we are capable of aligns with the reality of our skills and abilities. It's a solid and balanced sense of self, with neither inflating egotism nor diminishing self-doubt.

- *I am good enough and I can be better* is the mantra of humble confidence. *I am good enough* allows us to let go of any need to prove. *I can be better* represents a quest to improve that's fuelled by a thirst for learning rather than a compulsion to compensate for something that we lack.

- Humble confidence cuts our self-doubt down to size, sloughing off the excess upon which the self-doubt tax is levied.

- There's an assurance that comes from the alignment of our confidence with our capability, which allows us to be comfortable with being our unique selves.

- Being clear on what matters to us can feed our confidence, as we gain assurance from seeing that our actions align with our values.

4

Faulty calibration

It's possible that you've heard 'you should be more confident!' many times from a colleague or friend. They go on to list your myriad strengths, but you can't believe them because your calibration is faulty. You don't see your strengths and your achievements as others see them – they look smaller to you. Worse than that, your weaknesses and your 'haven't done yets' look much bigger to you than they look to those around you. 'You should be more confident' is such a well-intentioned thing to say, full of appreciation and support. It's an exhortation from someone who sees your many strengths and wants to encourage you to see them too. But, unfortunately, it doesn't work. It implies that somehow confidence is a choice, that there's a switch that we could reach for to switch off self-doubt now that we know that we 'should' have confidence.

In this chapter, we'll explore and gently challenge your calibration of your capability, with the aim of diagnosing the fault and enabling you to match your level of confidence more closely with your level of capability (the definition of humble confidence). Along the way, we'll investigate the way that you hear feedback and consider how that might be contributing to your faulty calibration.

A hall of mirrors

On a family holiday to Suffolk a couple of years back, my daughter and I laughed at our reflections in the mirrors on Southwold Pier. Each mirror had a different distortion: one making us look very short and very wide; one elongating our bodies; one giving us a wibbly-wobbly appearance. If there's a fault in your calibration of your capabilities, it's possible that you have created your own version of these pier mirrors, leading you to see a distorted reflection of yourself.

Your strengths mirror will be like the mirror that makes your reflection smaller. You're not seeing the true extent of your strengths, which makes it impossible for you to own your strengths and tricky to fully utilize them. You may also look at your achievements in the same distorted mirror, minimizing them. *It was actually quite easy. Anyone could have done it. There was a lot of luck really. It was largely down to Kate.* It may be that you quickly put achievements behind you, immediately turning your attention to the next big thing. It's difficult, even impossible, for you to pause and acknowledge what you have achieved and to absorb the success that could fuel confidence. Perhaps you could create for yourself the equivalent of the warning that appears on car wing mirrors: the objects in the mirror are closer than they appear. Perhaps there is somewhere you could capture your own reminder to self: my strengths are bigger than they appear to me, and my achievements are more significant than I might lead myself to believe.

When you come to consider your weaknesses, you move along the pier to a different mirror altogether. Here you stand in front of the mirror that makes you look like a giant. Someone asks you to tell them about your weaknesses – it's no problem at all as you have lots; they are all on the tip of your tongue and you will happily reel them off. This might be, in part, a defence mechanism whereby you get in first with your self-criticism in order to take the sting out of any negative feedback that might be about to come your way. Subconsciously, you might decide to go in hard on yourself because it's much more bearable to hear other people talk you up, telling you that you're not all that bad. You don't believe them (because you're too attached to your distorted view of yourself), but it's still better than taking the risk of saying 'I'm good at this' and then having others disagree.

An uncertain grasp

For some people, the mirrors aren't distorted in quite the same way; it's more nuanced than small strengths and big weaknesses. I come across coaching clients who have a seemingly contradictory relationship to their expertise. On the one hand, they are proud of their expertise, fully aware of the knowledge that they have built and the experience they have gained; there's a justifiable sense of pride. And yet, on the other hand, there's the absence of a full sense of trust in themselves. They know their capability and yet they don't always trust themselves to be able to access it.

My coaching client Amy is an excellent finance leader. One of the strands of our coaching work was to decode Amy's formula for confidence. She could see that she had delivered significant steps forward for the function that she led, and yet she easily slipped into a trough of self-doubt when she was faced with something new. What Amy held on tightly to was a model of confidence based on proof and data. 'I only know that I can do something if I have done it before. In order to feel confident about an upcoming task, I need to have evidence that I've successfully done it before.' This need for proof that she could do it before she felt confident meant that she could only ever feel sure of herself when she was repeating something. There was an obvious downside to this model of confidence: novel challenges and new tasks are unavoidable.

Attaching confidence to experience-based proof makes it especially difficult to change role or change organization. Amy considered changing organization for a number of years. Whilst there were some strong threads connecting her to her employer, the biggest reason why it took her a long time to take the step from wanting to leave to handing in her resignation was the fear of how she would feel. Amy knew her confidence formula and she knew therefore that choosing to leave an organization where she'd spent six years was going to mean stepping into an abyss of self-doubt. She knew that she would then have to begin the long (and sometimes exhausting) process of reconvincing herself of her capability as she painstakingly proved that she could deliver success in a new organization. The focus of our work together was to support Amy to develop a new confidence formula: *I only know that I can do something if I have done it before* became *I can draw on my wide-ranging experience to date as I take on new things*. With this more solid sense of her capabilities, Amy made the move and is flourishing in her new organization.

Owning your strengths

With my coaching clients, I sometimes notice that the process of taking ownership of their strengths is uncomfortable, as they battle with programming from their childhood such as *no one likes a show-off* or *real talent is quiet – if you're good, you don't need to blow your own trumpet*. If you notice a similar discomfort in yourself, these ways of thinking might help to alleviate it. They are useful thoughts when considering your strengths.

- I'm better able to access and use my strengths if I'm clear about what they are.
- I can be brilliant at something and still have room to improve.

- Acknowledging a strength does not trigger complacency.
- Acknowledging how good I am at one thing is not the same as claiming to be good at everything.
- Acknowledging a strength is a statement of truth, not boasting.

In Chapter 3, you completed Coach Yourself Confident #12 called *I am good enough*. The intention behind that exercise was to support you to see your strengths clearly. This kind of reflective work is a first step on the way to really owning and feeling good about your strengths. I'm going to invite you to build on that activity now.

COACH YOURSELF CONFIDENT #15

 REFLECTION: Owning your strengths

Step 1

Go back to the notes that you made when you completed Coach Yourself Confident #12 – I *am good enough*, and read out what you wrote as ways to complete the sentence: 'When I am at my best, I…'. It might sound odd, but I'd like you to read this out loud. You don't have to read it to someone else, just read it aloud to yourself – there's a difference between hearing it in your head and hearing it out loud.

Step 2

Now reflect: As you read out your strengths, were you aware of any reluctance to fully acknowledge or own them?

If so, I invite you to take a bit of time with the bullet points that I offered as useful thoughts when considering your strengths (in the section above – 'Owning your strengths'). Read through the bullet points slowly, noticing if any of the thoughts that I've offered trigger resistance or discomfort in you. Where this happens, I encourage you to stay with that bullet point for a few moments. Read the thought again and see if you can sit with the possibility that it might be true.

Step 3

Now repeat Step 1 and notice whether anything is beginning to shift in your relationship to your strengths. Did it feel at all different second time round?

Feedback through a filter

So far in this chapter we've focused on how you see yourself, as this has a direct impact on your level of confidence. It's likely that your confidence is also impacted by the views that others have of you. This is a meaty topic, and we'll explore much more about the implications of allowing our confidence to be shaped by others as part of Chapter 7: Homegrown confidence. Here I invite you to consider your response to feedback, with a particular focus on whether you're able to hear feedback clearly or whether your calibration of feedback from others has a fault.

In my experience, many of those who lack confidence hear feedback through a filter. How does that filter work? Well, when we are given feedback, we hold it up against our self-image to see if it fits. If the feedback doesn't fit with how we see ourselves, with how we evaluate our own capabilities, then it's difficult for us to process it. If our confidence lags behind our capability, positive feedback bounces off, unprocessed and unabsorbed because we can't square it with how we see ourselves. I still have to watch out for my response to positive feedback, being careful not to let my 'that's so kind' default response kick in. Yes, it may be that it is kind that someone has taken the time to offer appreciative feedback to me, but the kindness doesn't go further than that. For years my verbalized 'that's so kind' was actually understood inside my head as 'that's so kind that they would make something up to try to make me feel good.' No, they're not making it up to make me feel better; they're seeing something real and appreciating it.

I see clients who have well-developed defences for positive feedback. They resist, discount and sidestep positive evaluations. In the words of one client: 'I don't absorb positive feedback, so I don't get a boost from that... but negative feedback? Well, I *really* hear that, and I can go into a tunnel of self-criticism.' The gates are closed tightly against positive feedback, but they are thrown wide open for any hint of negative feedback. The reason we hear negative feedback really loudly if we're lacking confidence is that it fits only too well with our harsh, part-formed self-image. I see myself as lacking, therefore any critical feedback chimes with my own view. I hear the feedback and I accept it as true because it reinforces my own sense of what I lack.

A couple of years ago, I participated in Steve Chapman and Simon Cavicchia's brilliant programme Playing at the Edge: Creative Adventures with the Inner Critic.[22] Steve suggested that someone criticizing us only hurts if our inner critic agrees. Or to put it another way, that it's a game of 'shit snap'. If someone has a criticism of us and we also hold that card about ourselves, that's a moment of shit snap that really hurts. If you have a particularly harsh and active inner critic, then you might hold a lot of critical cards about yourself, meaning that there's plenty of opportunity for shit snap.

COACH YOURSELF CONFIDENT #16

 REFLECTION: A feedback filter?

For this activity, I'm inviting you to do something that may feel difficult: to request feedback. My intention is that you use this as a way to identify your feedback filters, and then to practice bypassing those filters, allowing you to draw the full benefit that comes from well-intentioned and thoughtful feedback.

---

[22] You can find details of Playing at the Edge at www.canscorpionssmoke.com

Step 1: Gather feedback

Choose three or four trusted colleagues, people who see the work that you do and who have your back. Ask these colleagues to offer feedback to you. You could use the three simple questions below:

1. What do you appreciate about my contribution at work?
2. What do you see as my key strengths? (Please say a little about the impact of each one.)
3. If you were to suggest one thing I could do in order to increase my effectiveness, what would it be? (Please say a little about the reason behind your suggestion, and the difference you think that it would make.)

I suggest that you ask for the feedback in written form – so that you can read it multiple times in order to really try to take it in. If a colleague prefers to give their feedback verbally, you could ask their permission to record the conversation so that you can listen to it again.

Step 2: Consider the feedback

Read (or listen to) the feedback two or three times and notice your response. Specifically, reflect on:

- How do you feel as you read the answers to questions 1 and 2? Do you recognize what your colleagues say about you? Do you notice yourself resisting it or discounting it in any way?

If you do notice yourself resisting or discounting, try reading the feedback out loud to yourself, phrasing it in a way that takes ownership for the feedback. For example, if Katherine told you: 'I value your ability to simplify complex ideas', you would say aloud to yourself: 'Katherine values my ability to simplify complex ideas.'

- How do you feel as you read the answers to question 3? Is your response similar or different to the feelings evoked by reading the first two questions? What shows up in your response – shame, discomfort, curiosity, recognition, interest, excitement? A mixture of feelings?

Try getting really curious about what your colleagues have suggested. And if you're noticing discomfort or shame, try reading the suggestions aloud to yourself prefaced by 'I could be even more effective if…'. (The word 'even' is important here because it frames the suggestion as an opportunity to develop further as opposed to the identification of a deficit to address.)

The highest of bars

There's another issue with calibration: faulty calibration of 'enough', both in the sense of what standard of performance is good enough and in the sense of what volume of work is enough. A former coaching client, Kerry, said to me: 'I just want to do a phenomenal job.' I was immediately struck by her choice of word; she didn't want to do a good job, or even a great job, she wanted her contribution to be phenomenal. That's a high bar and one that I find exhausting to even contemplate. On individual projects, Kerry struggled to see the bar that matched what the business needed. Instead of getting really clear on the minimum viable product, Kerry's default was to shoot for the stars, to go after the maximum possible product. This was not about business need, but about Kerry's internal need to over-deliver in order to believe that she was deserving of her director level role.

For Arjun, a regional managing director for a high-end technology manufacturer, missing targets in the financial year 2020–21 was a reflection of his lack of capability. He was fully aware of the extent of the earthquake in the market as a result of the Covid-19 pandemic. He was fully aware of the downturn for the whole sector and for all of his competitors, and yet Arjun couldn't unhook himself from the internal narrative that said *I should have responded more quickly. I should have been more creative. I should have found a way to make up the shortfall in sales.* It's important for leaders to feel a sense of ownership for their part of the organization, but if this ownership is overplayed, it can become a form of self-aggrandizing, a fantasy of super-human capability. *If I were capable, I would be able to deliver the targets.* This belief becomes untethered from the reality of the context.

Arjun's confidence, his view of his own capability, was tightly wrapped up around the business results that his organization delivered. He was hooked by the fantasy that *If I were capable, I would be able to deliver the targets.* His default was to blame himself, to look inside for a reason for missed targets, rather than to look outside at the context. Missed targets triggered catastrophizing, as he lost faith in himself and assumed that the parent organization would lose faith in him too. It took a conversation with the CEO to resettle Arjun, a conversation in which the CEO was helpfully unequivocal: 'No one could have hit those targets. We know you will rebuild. We trust you.' I worked with Arjun to see if he could give himself permission to let go of his unreasonable expectations of himself, to recalibrate his sense of what 'ought to be' possible.

We unearthed a fear in our work together, and it turned out to be pivotal to Arjun's attempts to recalibrate. Arjun could see that his expectations of himself were unreasonable, but he feared that if he let go of those expectations, he would tumble all the way to the opposite end of the spectrum, to the territory of excuses and sloping shoulders. This is the trap of binary thinking, and it's an easy trap to fall into. The truth is, however, that Arjun – or any leader who habitually takes an unrealistic level of ownership – would have to shift dramatically to become a 'not my fault' leader. With support, Arjun was able to recognize that such a dramatic shift was unlikely and that it was certainly not the inevitable consequence of unhooking from his fantasy of super-human capability.

Similar to perfectionism, a badly calibrated sense of what constitutes enough – an aspiration to be phenomenal – sets up a dispiriting focus on the gap. Your attention is continuously focused on what hasn't been achieved rather than what has, and your evaluation of your performance is skewed by the sheer audaciousness of your expectation of yourself. Phenomenal is an unreachable bar. The bar needs to be stretching yet attainable, not completely out of reach. I was really struck by this point when I spoke to Chris Fawkes, weather forecaster and broadcaster on the BBC. He was crystal clear on the question of reasonable expectations and an appropriately high bar. 'The nature of forecasting is that we're trying to predict something that's unknown. We use some of the biggest supercomputers on the planet, and even with all of that technology behind you, sometimes the weather has different ideas. You can do your absolute best, be really thorough and use all of your skills and experience, and sometimes you just can't get it right. Sometimes the weather will do something unexpected. It's not possible to perfectly predict the future.'

Chris has high standards, strives to do his best every day and is passionate about continuing to learn. What he doesn't have is an unhelpfully high bar against which to measure himself. He combines a commitment to doing the best job he can with a pragmatic acceptance that it's impossible to forecast the weather (or anything) with absolute precision. This blend of passion and pragmatism enables him to be realistic in his expectations of himself. Chris talked about when things go wrong: 'I try my hardest. And if something unexpected does happen, I always look back to see if I could have done something differently.' There's disappointment, but instead of beating himself up, Chris gets curious.

So far, we've talked about setting the bar at an appropriate height. The bar also needs to be the right bar. 'A key light bulb moment for me was realizing that I did not need to have all the answers. I've realized that the more seasoned and senior I've become in my career, having the answers becomes less important. Collaborating, inviting alternate ways of thinking and seeking out different points of view is a combination that makes for much better results!' These were the words of my former colleague, Kim Stokes, as she reflected on the upward shift in her confidence over the course of a 20-year career. Having all the answers feels intimidating and difficult, whereas building relationships and collaborating feels much more accessible. While Kim's bar was a bar of expertise, knowledge and answers, she constantly felt like she was falling short. When she swapped that for a bar of relationship and collaboration, she was able to see that she more than measured up. Her confidence grew because she changed her perspective on what good leadership looks like. We might not realize it, but we set bars for ourselves all the time, and these bars are held up by 'shoulds'. What Kim did was let go of a belief that leaders should have all of the answers.

COACH YOURSELF CONFIDENT #17

 REFLECTION: Question every 'should'

What 'shoulds' might you be holding onto? Try bringing to mind a situation in which you lack confidence and see if you can identify any 'should' that might be at play. The examples below are offered as a way to stimulate your thinking and to help you to pinpoint your 'should'.

Examples:

I feel unsure of myself in meetings because while I'm getting things straight in my mind, others are jumping in with their point of view.	Leaders **should** be able to give immediate and clear answers.
I'm introverted and feel uncomfortable in large group settings.	Leaders **should** be outgoing and charismatic.
I'm more about data than blue sky thinking.	Strategy **should** be fuelled by 'out there' big picture thinking.
I'm not great with numbers – I have to work hard on my understanding of the P&L.	Exec members **should** find the numbers easy.

Once you've identified that a 'should' is at play, investigate it and really try to get forensic. Where did it come from? Does the 'should' belong to you – it's something that you believe – or have you absorbed an organizational norm? Is it reasonable? Perhaps try forming an argument against your 'should'.

The longest of lists

There's a seemingly simple skill that I am yet to master. I am completely unable to write a realistic to-do list. There are occasional days when I complete everything that is on my list, but these are few and far between, and much more frequently I end the day with a small feeling of disappointment. Even when I have achieved a lot, there's a lingering sense of discomfort about the items on the list that remain undone. It's not my commitment to hard work that's the issue, nor an inability to focus, nor an issue of taking on tasks for which I don't have the requisite skill. It's an issue of calibration. What I appear to be unable to do is to calibrate what is realistic for me to achieve within the time that I have. Instead of a focused to-do list, what I end up with is more like an extended wish list of all the things that would be great to get done if I could somehow sidestep the constraints of time.

One of the tactics I have tried to help me to calibrate better is to buy a to-do pad that sets out different categories for the day. Each sheet is headed 'Today's plan of attack' and below are three sections: 'most critical' (with space for six tasks), 'would be nice' (with space for four tasks) and 'not a chance' (with space for two tasks).[23] Unfortunately, the 'today's plan of attack' post-it has not proved to be the solution to my faulty calibration of daily capacity. I have no complaints about the stationery. It's well-designed; it looks pleasing and it cleverly asks for focus and realism. My issue is one of user error. I do write things in all of the sections, but my mind chooses to ignore the headers, meaning that I just extend the 'most critical' section to the entire post-it, which completely misses the point. In doing so, I deprive myself of the genuine satisfaction if I were to tick off a 'would be nice' task. And I deprive myself of the psychological balm of being able to

---

[23] Copyright 2015 Knock Knock LLC

see (and believe) that the tasks I didn't get done were not absolutely necessary for that day's work.

If you have a similarly tricky relationship with your to-do list, then you will know that it can erode your confidence. The unrealistic list sets up an inevitable failure to complete and can trigger self-criticism: *If I was better at my job / smarter / more focused, I could get everything done.* To avoid this daily erosion of confidence, we need to shift our relationship with the list. I'd like to offer you a practice that might help – switching the process on its head and capturing what's complete rather than what's outstanding.

COACH YOURSELF CONFIDENT #18

 PRACTICE: A done list

Create a 'done list' for yesterday. Include everything that you achieved, large and small. Include everything, especially those unexpected things that popped up and had to be dealt with.

Read back through your list and notice how your done list makes you feel. If it helps you to view your day with balance and objectivity; this is a quick practice that you could use every day.

I know that I'm not alone in my inability to calibrate capacity in a realistic way. And sometimes the consequence is one that is far more significant than my niggling feeling of disappointment: it's burnout. Too often I see leaders who have to-do lists that run to multiple pages, alongside a back-to-back calendar and an overflowing inbox. And their response to this overwhelming quantity of work? *I should be able to get through it.* Should they? It's possible that there are wins to be had in terms of focus, planning and organization. Perhaps there's an opportunity to empower their team to a greater extent. Those things might make some difference, but for most self-doubt taxpayers they are unlikely to be enough because sitting beneath the *I should be able to do it* is often the even more insidious *If I were any good at this job, I would be able to keep up*; the assumption that the fault lies within them.

This is self-doubt interfering with the ability to calibrate workload, to calibrate what a strong level of contribution would look like: What is enough? What is unreasonable? What is super-human and unsustainable? If you interpret the fact that the requirement of the role can't be met within the hours available as *I'm not good enough*, then you fall into the trap of just working harder and harder. You take on more and more because you *should* be able to do it. You are reluctant to flag the issue, to signal that you're becoming overworked and exhausted, because this would draw attention to your inability; after all, *you should be able to get through it.* Boundaries collapse, hours become longer and your energy is sapped. And you're a willing victim because you have told yourself that maintaining boundaries is a sign that you can't cope or that you're not good enough.

If you find yourself in this situation, then a reality check is desperately needed. The next practice offers some ways to do that.

COACH YOURSELF CONFIDENT #19

 ## PRACTICE: A reality check for 'I should be able to get through it'

Below are three things that you could try – different ways to calibrate your workload and to test the validity of a belief that 'I should be able to get through it.'

Another pair of eyes

Ask someone to help you calibrate your workload. It could be someone (inside or outside your work) who can bring objectivity and analytical skill. Or, if you work within an organization, you may be able to approach an HR person with expertise in role design.

Gather data

What could you map out that would help to bring some objectivity to your assessment of your workload? Examples might include:

- Number of direct reports and how this compares to peers in the organization.
- Number of strategic priorities that you are leading.
- Number of strategic priorities that you are supporting.
- Budgetary responsibility.
- Hours per week / month in key meetings.
- Number of emails / instant messages per day.

If you work for yourself, the data might look different – perhaps you could try creating a spreadsheet of all of your client commitments, along with a realistic estimate of the hours of work involved for each element of work.

Take the opposite perspective

Work with the hypothesis that there is simply too much work. Begin a justification for additional resource – how would you make the case? You may or may not put forward the resource request, the idea of taking this perspective is to help you to view your workload through a lens undistorted by a sense that you should be able to get through it.

To sum up...

- Our lack of confidence can stem from a distortion in the way that we see ourselves. Our strengths and achievements look smaller to us than they do to others, whilst our weaknesses are magnified in our minds.

- Consciously acknowledging and owning our strengths and achievements can help to bring them into more realistic focus. Addressing the distortion that makes our strengths seem small is part of what reduces the gap between our confidence and our capability.

- When we hear feedback, we hold it up against our self-image. If we're hard on ourselves, we can find it difficult to absorb positive feedback, so we deny ourselves the confidence boost that internalized positive feedback could provide.

- As self-doubt taxpayers, we're more able to absorb negative feedback because it chimes with how we see ourselves, reinforcing our own sense of what we lack.

- Lack of confidence can undermine our ability to calibrate what is 'enough', both in the sense of what standard of performance is good enough and in the sense of what volume of work is enough.

5

Confidence saboteurs

Confidence can be tricky to pin down. Sometimes it's present and at other times our confidence deserts us, without warning. Sometimes our mind is calm and focused on the challenge in front of us and sometimes we're filled with doubt that we're up to the task. If we are to grow a robust and enduring feeling of confidence, we need to understand our confidence saboteurs. We need to understand what can drain our self-belief at the very moment that we need it and what can erode confidence over time.

'I decry the injustice of my wounds, only to look down and see that I am holding a smoking gun in one hand and a fistful of ammunition in the other.' These wise words from counsellor and author Craig D. Lounsbrough are apt for our exploration of confidence saboteurs. All too often we unintentionally diminish our own confidence. Most of the saboteurs that we'll consider in this chapter have something in common – they exist in our own head. I say this not to diminish the very real impact that they have, nor to attribute any kind of blame. I say it to reflect the reality of how confidence works and to offer encouragement. The fact that these saboteurs work within the confines of your mind means that you can take control. You can adjust your ways of thinking; it's not easy, but it's possible. And in doing so, you can tackle the saboteurs and claim your confidence.

The suspects we're focusing on in this chapter are the inner critic, comparisonitis, fear of other people's opinions, overthinking, perfectionism, fear of failure and tiredness (which usually has its friend, 'the voice of doom', tagging along). In addition, we'll take a look at how other people can undermine our self-belief. My invitation to you is to take the opportunity to dig into your own confidence saboteurs and to try out the simple *Coach Yourself Confident* practices that will help you to keep those saboteurs in check.

The inner critic

There are times when our confidence deserts us at a time when we need it most, when we're stepping into a situation in which it's important that we do ourselves justice. The stakes might be high because of the people who are there. Senior HR Director at Kellanova, Ben Lamont, reflected on the way that his respect for hierarchy impacts his confidence: 'I experience fleeting drops of confidence when I'm in meetings with senior people. It's a fleeting sense of "what the hell am I doing here? This is the moment when they're going to find me out." And then after a few minutes, I'm able to see that my response is ridiculous and settle myself.' It's not only the seniority of the other attendees that can raise the stakes for a meeting. The stakes might be high because of the significance of the outcome you're targeting: project sign-off, additional funding, a promotion, a pay increase. Or the stakes might be high because the setting brings with it a high degree of visibility, perhaps presenting to a large audience or being filmed. These sorts of high-stakes situations often represent an irresistible invitation for the inner critic.

In Chapter 2, we explored how the harsh commentary of the inner critic can contribute to your payment of the self-doubt tax. I invited you to work with ways to distance yourself from your inner critic because establishing a bit of distance from that internal voice enables you to choose how to respond to what it is telling you. Without wanting to give too much of a starring role to the pesky inner critic, it really does also need to appear here as we consider in-the-moment confidence dips. You might be familiar with the experience of an inner critic hijack; just at the moment when you need to access your confidence, your inner critic turns up the volume on its commentary and focuses on every possible reason to doubt yourself. As I reflect on my corporate career, I had many inner critic hijacks, often ahead of meetings where I was sharing a proposal with a group of more senior colleagues. I found a simple practice that helped to calm my nerves and clarify my thinking in those moments: truth telling.

At the heart of this practice is the recognition that the perspective of your inner critic is driven by fear and that what your inner critic tells you is not fact. There are flaws in the thinking and often a lack of evidence for the assertions that your inner critic makes. It can help to adopt the position of a neutral onlooker, capturing an evidence-based perspective on the situation. To do this, you notice what your inner critic is telling you and then identify what's true to say.

COACH YOURSELF CONFIDENT #20

 PRACTICE: Truth telling

Draw two columns on a piece of paper. In the left-hand column, write down what your inner critic is telling you. Don't edit what you hear in your head – there's no right or wrong here, just write down what your inner critic is saying.

Then in the right-hand column, take each of your inner critic's statements in turn and look at it really objectively. Is what your inner critic is saying an objective truth? If not, what are the truths to be noted down?

The word 'truth' is important here. You're not looking for banalities (everything will be OK) or false optimism (it will be brilliant!), but facts.

What my inner critic has to say	Truths
I should have done more preparation.	I've spent two hours pulling together the deck. There's no more that I can do now. No one else in the room has spent as long on the topic in preparation for this meeting.
They'll wonder why on earth they gave me this job in the first place.	This is not a performance evaluation.
If I can't answer a question, my credibility will be shot.	I have no way of knowing what the response will be if I can't answer a question. I have done my preparation and I have tried to anticipate what might be asked, so I am as prepared as I can be. If I can't answer something, I will commit to following up as soon as I can. My credibility is based on much more than how this one meeting goes.

Over time, the truth telling process becomes easier because you are likely to find recurring themes in what your inner critic says to you, and you become more adept at identifying what is true. At this point, you may no longer need to see the truths written down; it may be enough to simply notice and mentally counter your inner critic's untruths as you step into a situation which requires your most confident self. As themes become evident to you, you might be able to develop some simple mantras for yourself, for example, *I've done what I've done and can do no more.*

Comparisonitis

Our inner critics are often very interested in others, specifically in noticing and signposting all of the ways in which they are better than we are. They like nothing more than triggering the painful feeling of comparisonitis. It might be a made-up word that you won't find in a dictionary, but (sadly) the experience of comparisonitis is all too real. My habit of comparing myself to others and seeing myself as 'less than' is a longstanding one. My confidence took a blow when I moved from school to university and found myself amongst an incredibly able group of students on my history degree course. One student in particular became the focus of my comparisonitis: Esme. Quick thinking, eloquent and willing to speak out, Esme seemed to me to be everything that I wasn't, and I found her enormously intimidating. Alongside her in a seminar group, I didn't look at her and think *what a fantastic person to learn from.* No. Instead I thought *I'm nowhere near as good as her,* or on particularly bad days, *how the hell did I get here?*

In my coaching work, I come across three broad categories of comparisonitis: they are *more capable* than me (my belief about Esme), they are more *senior* than me and they are *different* to me. With all three, the comparison is unfavourable and diminishing: they are better than me. Let's unpack these three categories.

I coached Stefano, a commercial director who lost touch with his confidence during a time of high change within the executive team of which he was a part. His confidence was sabotaged by comparisonitis of the 'they are more capable than me' variety. Stefano described the colleagues who had recently joined him on the team as 'incredibly talented' and saw a multitude of ways in which these individuals were better than him. In his mind, Stefano created a composite of the perfect executive leader, made up of the best bits of all of his colleagues and used that as the profile against which to measure himself. Unsurprisingly, he came up short.

For a time, Stefano lost touch with himself. He disowned the fabulous strengths that had powered his career and fuelled the success of the business. He disowned the part that he had played in building the business, assigning that to the past – no longer relevant. And he became an avid collector of evidence to support his belief that he was 'less than' his colleagues. 'I'm just not as intelligent as the others. They are so sharp, so quick. They race through the agenda while I'm still formulating my thoughts.' As a result of this inner chatter (*I can't keep up with their thinking, they are just smarter than me*), Stefano stayed quiet, and the act of staying quiet reinforced his internal sense that his colleagues were better than him.

Our work together was about supporting Stefano to rediscover his place in that team, by correcting the harsh narrative he was telling himself and rebalancing his assessment of the strengths and qualities that he brought. It was about turning down the volume on comparisonitis and letting go of the idea that he had to match up to the best of the best. He did not have to be as good at data as the Director of Insights, he did not have to be as methodical as the Operations Director. After all, he had no expectation that his executive team colleagues must all match his ability to connect with customers and to put their needs at the very heart of business strategy. Stefano's comparisonitis was destructive, one-sided and diminishing. I applauded him when he found his own way to set it aside.

They are more *senior* than me... and therefore they are better than me / their perspective is more valuable than mine / they are more likely to be right than I am. These kinds of assumptions are all too commonly held, fed by the overt hierarchy that still characterizes the inner world of most organizations. There's a built in more-than / less-than language in the form of grades, which can feed an unhelpful organizational habit of deferring to the 'more thans' – the people higher up the organizational ladder. When I coach teams, I see the sunflower effect, where all heads – and attention – turn towards the most senior person in the room. I see self-censorship, where individuals try to anticipate what the senior person thinks instead of simply stating their own view. I see individuals staying small in relation to the more senior people around them, being overly respectful of hierarchy, and holding themselves back in the process.

They are *different* to me. Noticing differences can lead us to question ourselves. Rebecca Snow, Global HR Vice President for Mars Snacking told me: 'There are times when I feel that I'm wired quite differently from a lot of people in the business, so when I come into contact with these people who don't get me, and I don't get them, that can be a trigger for self-doubt.' Noticing the difference is an invitation for comparison, a feeling of being 'less than' and a dent in confidence. And there can be a multiplying effect when this difference is combined with hierarchy: I am 'less than' because I'm wired differently, *and* I'm 'less than' because I'm junior. A mental assumption of cause and effect can be particularly diminishing; they are more senior *because* they are different. I won't progress here because I'm not like them.

Rebecca told me about the different wiring that she notices. Over the course of her career, she has been aware that she hasn't felt as excited as many of her colleagues have about hitting sales targets or being the number one brand. Whilst well aware of how critical sales volume and market share are to any consumer goods business, Rebecca points out that commercial performance is not the only measure of business success (a position which fortunately now many companies are adopting and driving). 'There have been times when I have wondered if I really belong in the corporate world because I've felt inspired by different things to many of my colleagues.' Attached to this observation seems to be a question: Am I supposed to be like those colleagues? And it's a question that carries risk. Answering yes might lead us to act a part – to pretend to be like those others, rather than truly being ourselves. This is exhausting. And it's underpinned by a confidence sapping thought: you can't succeed by being you. In Chapter 7, we'll explore the confidence boosting invitation to really be yourself.

COACH YOURSELF CONFIDENT #21

 PRACTICE: Different does not equal better

The issue with comparisonitis is not how we see the other person. The issue is what our view of the other person does to the way that we see ourselves. The purpose of this exercise is to take a close look at a live example of comparisonitis and to dismantle it. In the process, you will reset the way that you see yourself.

1. Bring to mind an individual who triggers a 'less-than' feeling in you and make a note of the ways in which you believe that this other person is better than you.

2. Now take another look at your notes and see if you can reframe the comparison you are making with no element of 'less than' or 'more than'. Instead your aim is to set out the ways in which you and the other person have complementary skills.

Satnam is so much more creative than me.	*becomes…*	*Satnam and I are good at thinking together. She generates lots of ideas and we work together to refine them and figure out how they could work in practice.*

I'll never be as sharp on the numbers as Kate.	becomes…	When we work together, I can rely on Kate to quickly spot any issues in the data. Kate knows that I bring the ability to really step back and find a new perspective.

FOPO

FOPO is the fear of other people's opinions, or to give its proper name: allodoxaphobia. Allodoxaphobic individuals are afraid of listening to feedback of any kind. Hearing someone express an opinion about them triggers sweaty palms, accelerated heart rate, rapid breathing and feelings of nausea. Whilst not many of us fear the opinion of others to quite the extent of a phobia, most human beings share a discomfort about being judged. After all, as human beings, we're wired to care about what others think of us. For early humans, not caring about others' reactions might have led to being ostracised or banished from the tribe; a dangerous position. For self-doubt taxpayers, the discomfort is heightened because we already have an inner critic who is overly alert to our shortcomings; we don't need additional critical voices. We really don't want (or need) other people to signpost our flaws, and our FOPO leads to us stepping back, avoiding disagreement and conflict, avoiding the spotlight.

It seems to me that there's a false assumption sitting beneath FOPO. The assumption that it's possible to be viewed positively by everyone we come across. That if we try hard enough, we can ensure that everyone has a good opinion of us. If we can let go of this fantasy, then perhaps it becomes easier to deal with the judgements of others, with critical feedback. At the end of the day, there's one opinion of you that matters more than the others: yours. Of course feedback is valuable, but it should be taken alongside your own opinions and feelings. We can care what other people think without fearing their judgement. If I think my book is brilliant and someone else thinks it's terrible, that's just a difference of opinion. They are not right. I am not right. Not everyone will like what I have written. That's inevitable. And it's OK.

We'll come back to the distinction between caring about what people think and fearing their judgement as part of Chapter 7.

Mindreading

You are presenting and Bradley on the front row yawns theatrically and rubs his face with his hands. *Oh my God. He's absolutely bored to tears by the appalling dirge of my presentation. Everyone else must feel the same.* The sabotage of confidence happens when you are convinced by your interpretation; when in that moment, you believe that you can read minds. It can feel like your certainty in yourself drops like a stone, an immediate response to what you think is someone's reaction. What you think it is, not what you know it to be. A reminder: unless someone tells you what they are thinking, there is no way that you can possibly know what is going through their mind. This truth can be hard to accept. So many of us believe that we have mystical powers, that we can discern the nuances of thought whirring round in someone else's head. We can pick up clues, of course we can. But we need to accept that we might be right, we might be wrong. None of us have the ability to read minds.

What's the antidote to confidence sapping mindreading? I'd suggest two. The first is to try to spot yourself doing it, which means being really aware that you (and all of us) have the capacity to make up stories in your mind and that these stories are not always true. Noticing and telling yourself 'I'm doing that mindreading thing again' might be enough to lessen the certainty that you attach to your interpretation. Perhaps Bradley on the front row is bored to tears, or perhaps he's just tired. Perhaps he is trying to undermine you, or perhaps that's just how he yawns. The first antidote to mindreading is to remind yourself that your interpretation might be wrong.

The second antidote is to ask the person to share what they're thinking instead of assuming that you know. In my example, you might not want to stop mid-presentation and demand to know why Bradley is yawning. But you could ask a more general check-in question of the audience. 'How's this working for you so far? Are you with me? Any requests of me at this point?' Scary? Yes. But this is an invitation for data that will be really useful to you, whatever form it takes. If the response is a resounding 'all good', then it will be easier to set aside your *Bradley-yawned-everyone-must-be-bored* story. If your invitation elicits some requests that you do things differently, then you have the chance to make changes in the moment.

Overthinking

Overthinking is the mental equivalent of running on a treadmill where we expend significant effort without moving forward at all, achieving only exhaustion. Whereas physically running on a treadmill provides a cardiovascular workout, the mental equivalent of overthinking brings with it no benefit. For many of us, our minds are partial to an overthinking workout when we're lying in bed. Unsurprisingly, research shows that overthinking makes it hard to fall asleep, sometimes fuelling some additional overthinking about how awful tomorrow will be if we don't manage to get some sleep!

Our mental running effort is usually focused on the past or on the future; overthinking isn't about the here and now. With a focus on the past, we expend energy in worry and regret about what we've done (or what we haven't done), about things we've said (or things we haven't said). We play film clips inside our heads, reliving situations over and over again. As we watch and rewatch the scenario, we offer our inner critic ample opportunity to spot errors of judgement or missed chances. Of course, looking back doesn't have to be punishing. A healthy practice of reflection in which we seek to make sense of what has happened and what we have learned is constructive. This kind of looking back can be a confidence builder if our focus is on what went well and on identifying the learnings for next time. In this way, it's an active process of learning that enables us to continuously improve our skill in navigating what work (and life) throws at us.

When we get caught up in future-focused overthinking, we might be gripped by nerves, or we might be seeking ways to control what has not yet happened. This time our mental cinema is showing trailers for what's coming up, often with multiple different versions of how a situation might play out. The future-focused overthinking cinema specializes in drama, drawing us in with nervous anticipation, anxiety and fear. This is not a calm, balanced (and useful) consideration of potential scenarios. At the extreme, it's a dread inducing form of self-torture.

Mindfulness can be an antidote to overthinking because it brings your attention to the present moment – rather than stepping back into the past or forward into the future, your focus is on the here and now. The next *Coach Yourself Confident* activity is a simple mindfulness practice. Why not take a few minutes to try it now, so that it will be part of your toolkit, ready for when you need it.

COACH YOURSELF CONFIDENT #22

 PRACTICE: Mindfulness

This exercise is called Five Senses.[24] It's a quick and easy way to counteract the confidence sabotaging effect of overthinking by bringing your attention to the present moment.

---

[24] https://positivepsychology.com/mindfulness-exercises-techniques-activities/

- Notice *FIVE* things that you can *SEE*... perhaps things that aren't always there, like a tree that's newly in blossom.

- Notice *FOUR* things that you can *FEEL*... they could include the texture of your shirt, the feeling of the breeze on your skin, the smooth surface of the table.

- Notice *THREE* things you can *HEAR*... tune into background noises such as the chirp of a bird, the hum of the refrigerator, the sounds of traffic.

- Notice *TWO* things you can *SMELL*... perhaps there's a smell of food cooking, or if you're outside you might notice the fresh smell in the air after a rain shower.

- Notice *ONE* thing you can *TASTE*... You could take a sip of a drink, chew a piece of gum, eat something or just notice the current taste in your mouth.

Perfectionism

High standards. Ambition. A drive to improve. A motivation to achieve.

All of these things can be useful. They can fuel success at school, university and work. Perfectionism is more than these things. It's high standards on steroids. It's an expectation of yourself that is unreasonable, unattainable. If my bar for success is that the thing I am doing must be perfect, then I am bound to fail. Perfect is an illusion and perfectionism is an affliction. 'Perfectionism is the voice of the oppressor, the enemy of the people. It will keep you cramped and insane your whole life.' These are the words of Anne Lamott in her New York Times bestseller, *Bird by Bird: Instructions on Writing and Life*.

This part of the book was perhaps the one that I found the most difficult to write. I know a lot about perfectionism. I know too much about it really, about how it feels from the inside. The issue was that my perfectionism had quite a strong point of view on this section about perfectionism. So I researched, I wrote notes, I played around with metaphors and with different ways of structuring the section, but what I didn't do was write. Instead, there was a series of increasingly elaborate forms of procrastination; things that I needed to do to ensure that this section would be good enough. More than good enough. Perfect. And through that *if I just think about it for a bit longer I'll be able to make it perfect* process, my faith in myself and in the whole book writing project was slipping. Did I really know enough about the topic? Did I have something to say? Would it be something that others would find useful? Was my thinking right? That last question was particularly thorny: I wanted to be right, even though I knew that 'right' was an impossible goal to set for myself. There is no such thing as a single, correct set of ideas about confidence.

That's how the perfectionism saboteur works: it crushes confidence because perfection is unattainable. The bar we set ourselves, and against which our inner critic measures us, is panic-inducingly high, and our focus is on the gap. We don't see what we have done and appreciate what's brilliant about it; we focus instead on what's not perfect. We focus on the gap between the reality and our imagined ideal, and we imagine that it is the result of our inadequacies. If we were better at strategy / baking / playing the oboe, then we would reach our inflated expectations – we would achieve perfection. As we battle to close the gap between our ideal and our reality, we work excessively hard. And we beat ourselves up; however fantastic your output, there's always something that could be better.

In her book *The Imposter Cure*, Jessamy Hibberd writes: 'Perfection might seem possible if you just try hard enough, work longer and do better, but it's really a mirage hovering temptingly just out of reach. You might push yourself on to this beautiful oasis, but what happens when you get there? There's nothing to see, or it turns out to be further away than you thought. Aiming for perfection means that you can never sit still and enjoy the place you are in right now; it stops you feeling content and encourages you to undervalue all you already have as not being enough.'[25] Pursuit of the illusion of perfection is a never-ending quest, and it can become an absurdity. A senior coaching client realized what he was doing when he set himself preposterously high standards for his work on a key strategic question that he was leading for the organization. 'I'm trying to find a perfect answer for something that there isn't an answer for,' he told me.

I cannot offer you a cure for perfectionism because no such thing exists. In fact, there would be a deep irony about trying

---

[25] Hibberd, 2019.

to find *the* antidote to perfectionism. Instead, I invite you to explore the idea of perfect (and imperfect) a little further. This exploration can help to loosen the hold of perfectionism.

Donald Winnicott was a paediatrician and psychoanalyst who specialized in relationships between parents and infants during the 1950s. He developed the phrase 'the good enough parent'. This 'good enough' position stood in contrast to the impossible ideal of a 'perfect' parent. Winnicott recognized that it's not possible for a caregiver to be empathic, available and immediately responsive at all times. And, more importantly, that 'perfect', 100% available parenting would stunt the baby's emotional development by depriving the infant of the opportunity to learn to tolerate feelings of discomfort, frustration or anger.

I like the way that the writers at The School of Life summarize Winnicott's idea of good enough parenting: 'No child… needs an ideal parent. They just need an OK, pretty decent, usually well intentioned, sometimes grumpy, but basically reasonable father or mother.'[26] I suggest that we extend the concept of a good enough parent to the idea of being a good enough human being. No human being can be an ideal human being, that very idea is a nonsense. The first result returned on my quick Google search on 'definition of perfect' was *having all the required or desirable elements, qualities or characteristics; as good as it is possible to be.* Is it just me, or is the idea of a person being 'as good as it is possible to be' simply laughable? They would be done, finished, complete, with no further room for learning or growth.

---

[26] De Botton and The School of Life, 2019.

Let's take the view that as human beings, we just need to be an OK, pretty decent, usually well intentioned, sometimes grumpy, but basically reasonable person. That sounds a bit more attainable than our imaginary perfect human, and it sounds like a better description of someone I'd actually like to sit next to at a dinner party. The 'good enough' human sounds much more interesting than the perfect version who has already done everything, learned everything, achieved everything and has all the answers. That imaginary perfect person sounds like a pain in the backside. I can be a 'good enough' human *and* I can hold the curiosity and desire necessary to fuel continued growth. This growth does not stem from a desire to fill a gap or make up for an absence, but because I hold the belief that there is always room to grow. I am enough as I am *and* I can continue to grow. You'll remember from Chapter 3 that this is a core tenet of my definition of humble confidence.

If perfectionism is an oppressor, then good-enough-ism is a liberator. If you are a perfectionist, I urge you to consider how you might make friends with good enough. I'm well aware that you might be underwhelmed by this suggestion. You might judge it unoriginal, and as a committed perfectionist, you might see it as a misnomer. How can anything less than perfection be good enough? How can striving for anything less than the absolute best be good enough? How can that possibly be acceptable? I empathize with that reaction because despite an ongoing battle with my perfectionism over the course of three decades, I still sometimes shudder at the idea of lowering my expectations. Let's see if we can work through the discomfort together. Let's see if we can begin to (really) make friends with good enough.

One of the best book titles I have come across is John-Paul Flintoff's *A Modest Book About How to Make an Adequate Speech*. The title is so deliberately under-stated as to be intriguing. As an American reviewer (Jay Heinrichs) said: 'Where I come from, where modesty is a sin, Flintoff's book would be called *The Indispensable Guide to Giving an Unforgettable Speech*.' Which version of the title elicits confidence (I think I could do that) and which hooks your inner critic? For me, 'adequate' seems much more within reach than 'unforgettable'. Adequate is good enough. I like author Seth Godin's definition of perfect because the way that Godin frames perfect focuses on adequate rather than unforgettable. 'Perfect doesn't mean flawless. Perfect means it does exactly what I need it to do.' That's worth reading again: perfect means it does exactly what I need it to do.

This suggests a to-do in our quest to make friends with good enough: when we embark on a piece of work, we need to be crystal clear on what we need it to do. We need to get really clear on the spec: what exactly is the goal? We need to answer the question: with this piece of work, what is good enough? I recognize that there will be times when you want to exceed the spec on a particular piece of work. That's understandable, and it's OK *as long as you are making a conscious choice to do so*. We're not seeking to just lower our standards; we're seeking to use more precision in choosing how we invest our limited energies. The aim is to focus on the achievement of good enough, not on the achievement of perfection.

If you're familiar with perfectionism as one of your confidence saboteurs, give the next *Coach Yourself Confident* activity a try. It's an exercise in focusing on the achievement of good enough.

COACH YOURSELF CONFIDENT #23

 PRACTICE: Get clear on good enough

I invite you to try getting clear on good enough for a current piece of work.

1. Think about a specific piece of work that's underway or coming up.

2. What's the goal for this piece of work? What does it need to do?

3. Write down a set of bullet points to articulate what good enough delivery looks like for this piece of work, ensuring that everything that you write down is absolutely needed to achieve the stated goal; don't allow yourself anything that is above and beyond.

4. If you're struggling to do this, start by writing down what the ideal, perfectionism-tinged version of success looks like and then give yourself permission to edit it.

5. Read through your good enough spec and notice how it feels. Ask yourself, can I get comfortable with aiming for good enough on this particular deliverable?

There's a paradox embedded within perfectionism. We seek to avoid the possibility of failure by pursuing perfection, but perfect is just an illusion. In pursuing perfection, we are setting ourselves an unattainable target against which we will inevitably fall short. We might produce work that has touches of brilliance, but we will still fail to meet our goal. The pursuit of perfection is an uphill battle, one that can never be won because life is imperfect and human beings are imperfect. Mistakes, failure and loss are all inevitable, and that's where we're turning our attention next.

Fear of failure

I've kept hold of a newspaper article for a few years. The headline is 'Oh well done, class, you are all total flops' and the story tells of Wimbledon High School holding a festival to teach pupils how to learn from failure and come out stronger. The Failure Week was held to teach pupils that they would not always win in life and to help them learn how to make the most of defeat. The emphasis was on having a go, rather than playing it safe and perhaps achieving less. In the words of the headteacher Heather Hanbury, 'My message to girls is that it is better to lead a life replete with disappointment than one where you constantly wonder "if only." For high achieving girls especially, where fear of failure can be crippling, this is vitally important.'

Fear of failure is a part of the human condition. We know how unpleasant the experience of failure can be so we seek to avoid it. Something doesn't go our way, what we expect to happen doesn't happen, things don't turn out as we'd hoped. We can feel disappointment, embarrassment, even shame.

Failure can be the perfect invitation for our inner critic to shout loudly about our inadequacies. We get stuck in a swirl of thoughts about what we could and should have done differently, catastrophizing about the consequences. It's not only the discomfort of failing against our own expectations that we wish to avoid. Possibly even worse is our failure being visible to others. If our inner critic has narrated the failure as being evidence of our innate uselessness, we fear that what others see is not this mistake, but rather our inadequacy, our uselessness laid bare. We may even hold a belief that others won't like us if we fail.

The fear of failure sabotages confidence by interrupting the very first step of the Confidence Momentum Cycle that we looked at in Chapter 1:

THE CONFIDENCE MOMENTUM CYCLE

We hold back instead of stepping forward and taking action. By letting the fear of failure stop us from doing something, we are stopping ourselves from accessing the learning, progress and potential success that the cycle offers. If we are to grow, then we need to fail, and that means building up our tolerance for failing, learning and moving forward. In our cycle, that's represented in the setback loop where things not going as we'd expected is learning, not failure.

Task one as we approach the territory of our relationship with mistakes and failure: face the unavoidable truth that we all screw-up. To be human is to mess up. In his book, *Creating a Life*, James Hollis says: 'Anyone with a modicum of consciousness and a mild dollop of integrity will be able to enumerate a very long list of screw-ups, shortcomings, betrayals, moments of cowardice and generalized incompetence. Anything less than a very long list suggests either an undeveloped awareness or an act of great self-deception.'[27] We all fail, and we've all heard the stories about failure as a step on the road to success. JK Rowling's manuscript was rejected 12 times, the Beatles were told that guitar groups were on their way out, Michael Jordan was dropped from his high school basketball team. We know that we all fail, but we don't *know* it. It's a bit like making friends with good enough: fine in theory but tricky in practice.

I suggest that we all consciously join the failure club, a club in which the first rule is that *you do talk about failure club*. The more we talk about failing, the more normal it will be. Talking about what goes wrong is a way to remind ourselves that it's possible to be at once insightful, intelligent, idiotic and impulsive. No one is *a failure* or *a success*, we're all doing our best with what we've got; we're figuring things out as we go.

---

[27] Hollis, 2001.

We can take this point further and say that the whole idea of success and failure is problematic because it's binary, implying that it's one or the other. In reality, there are so often shades in between. I forget a carefully rehearsed speech midway through and I'm forced to improvise. There's arguably a failure there – the forgetting – but the ability to improvise surely counts as a success? What feels like a failure now can turn out not to be. Or what feels like a disastrous mistake can turn out not to matter at all. There's probably a whole other book to be written on the paradigm of success or failure. For now, I'll content myself with looking at how we can avoid the fear of failure sabotaging our confidence. Let's get back to that idea of a failure club with an exercise for you to try.

COACH YOURSELF CONFIDENT #24

  PRACTICE: Talk about failure club

I invite you to play with an imaginary interview question: 'Tell me about a time when you failed.'

Talk out loud and try to be as animated and excited as you can. See if you can bring the same level of energy to your description as you would bring to an articulation of a big success.

You're not reliving the failure to beat yourself up or to stir up difficult emotions, but to extract the learnings – and to remind yourself that you survived.

Failure happens and we survive; failure is painful but not fatal. Acknowledging this truth can diminish the fear that the possibility of failure provokes. By reminding ourselves that we can survive failure, we make it easier to step forward and try. It might sound counter-intuitive, but I think a careful examination of the worst case scenario can be comforting because we realize that if the worst happened, we could get through it. That's the thought that sits behind the next practice: constructive pessimism.

COACH YOURSELF CONFIDENT #25

 PRACTICE: Try constructive pessimism

Think about an upcoming work situation about which you don't feel fully confident. Now bring to mind the worst case scenario, invite your inner critic to express their worst fears.

For example:

I'll forget all of the data points when I present to the Board. They will ask me questions and I'll just stand there open-mouthed, red-faced and shaking. The Chair will get so frustrated that she'll yell 'you're an idiot – get out!' I'll burst into tears and run out of the room.

Now consider two questions about your imagined worst case scenario:

1. Do you know that this will happen?
2. If it did happen, could you survive it?

I can be definitive about the answer to the first question: no. You absolutely cannot predict the future. How many times have you worried about what will happen and then been pleasantly surprised by reality?

And the second question: could you survive it? The question is not about whether it's desirable, or whether you'd prefer to avoid it, but could you survive it? If your imaginings were to become reality, would you find a way to get through it? I'm pretty certain that the answer is yes.

My final word on the topic of failure relates to language and the role that language can play in how we feel about ourselves. 'Failure' is one of those words that carries a lot of baggage. Perhaps it's because it takes us back to our school days when our work was marked. We either passed or we failed, and it mattered, or at least it certainly seemed to matter at the time. Psychology Professor Carol Dweck, the originator of the concept of growth mindset, talks about a high school in Chicago where the students have to accumulate 84 units in order to graduate. But it's not pass or fail. It's pass or *not yet*.[28] That simple change in terminology is really significant. Fail feels definitive and carries with it the risk of being translated into *I am a failure*. *Not yet* is less definitive, suggesting a current position on the learning curve rather than a final judgement of ability. *Not yet* is a moment in time with an inbuilt suggestion of possibility. I haven't achieved it *yet*, but I might achieve it in the future. I can achieve it in the future. I will achieve it in the future.

You can easily harness the power of *yet*. Read the sentences below and notice the difference made by the word yet. Three letters. It's a small, but mighty word.

> I can't do this.
> I can't do this *yet*.

> It doesn't make sense to me.
> It doesn't make sense to me *yet*.

> I'm not confident in the executive board meeting.
> I'm not *yet* confident in the executive board meeting.

Tiredness

In considering the confidence saboteurs, we can't miss out tiredness and its good friend the 'voice of doom'. Tiredness and worry combine to create the perfect conditions for overthinking and can act as an irresistible invitation to our inner critic. When I was growing up, my mum used

---

[28] Dweck, 2014. Available at: www.youtube.com/watch?v=hiiEe MN7vbQ (accessed 9 May 2023).

to refuse to talk to me about things that were troubling me late at night, insisting that things would look better in the morning. It could be frustrating at the time, but she was absolutely right. When we are tired, everything seems disproportionately challenging and our belief in ourselves is reduced. The issue appears bigger, and our capacity to resolve it appears smaller – cue a sharp drop in confidence.

It turns out that my mum's instinct is backed up by research; sleeping difficulties are correlated with lower self-confidence.[29] If we can calm our minds sufficiently to be able to drop off, then sleep can make an enormous difference to the narrative in our head, and often things do look better in the morning. The unconscious workings of our mind during the night have created a bit of distance from the issue; it no longer looks quite so big. There's another aspect too; the cumulative impact of punishing hours put in by those of us who are paying the self-doubt tax in the form of overwork. It's a downward spiral; we exhaust ourselves as we use hard work and excessive effort to compensate for our lack of confidence, then the exhaustion serves to undermine our sense of what we're capable of. Down and down we go.

The best thing to do if we find ourselves in this spiral is obvious, but not always easy to do: stop, rest, sleep. Self-doubt taxpayers are often well practised at pushing on through. They can force themselves to keep working, chasing the mirage of being 'on top of things', telling themselves that they will be able to relax when this next thing is done. This capacity to keep going can feel good in the short term; it

---

[29] Lemola et al., 2013.

helps to feed the appetite for task completion as evidence of being good enough, but it's not sustainable. Ultimately, there's a risk of burnout if we don't allow ourselves the essential practice of resting and recharging. There are rich resources available on the web if you are struggling with sleep, and if you're suffering with chronic sleeplessness, then please seek medical help. Sleep is not the only form of rest, and I'm offering the practice below as a way to spark your thinking about how much attention you pay to a conscious process of recharging your batteries.

COACH YOURSELF CONFIDENT #26

 PRACTICE: Rest and recharge

According to physician and researcher, Dr Saundra Dalton-Smith, there are seven forms of rest, each of which are important in enabling you to recharge yourself.[30] I invite you to read through these brief descriptions of the different forms of rest and to note down three things:

1. The forms of rest that already form part of your routine.
2. One form of rest to which you'd like to pay more attention.
3. A simple experiment that you'll try.

---

[30] Dalton-Smith, 2021. Available at https://ideas.ted.com/the-7-types-of-rest-that-every-person-needs (accessed May 2023).

Physical rest can be passive or active. Passive physical rest includes sleeping, while active physical rest means restorative activities such as yoga or running.

Mental rest is about regularly switching off your busy brain, perhaps through short breaks during the working day or mindfulness practice.

Sensory rest provides a reprieve from the stimulation of screens and interactions and might be 60 seconds with your eyes closed at your desk or a no-screen hour before bed.

Creative rest comes from connecting to sources of inspiration, be that by appreciating nature or by enjoying art, music, architecture.

Emotional rest means being able to pay attention to, and express, how you're feeling. It entails paying attention to your own needs instead of people pleasing.

Social rest is the result of spending time with people whose company you find energizing or nurturing.

Spiritual rest comes from feeling that you're part of something bigger than yourself, perhaps practicing a religious faith, involvement in the community or meditation.

I want to give the final word in this section on tiredness to my friend, entrepreneur Dr Carrie Goucher. Carrie has a simple '11–7' rule that you might want to adopt. She told me: 'I don't pay attention to thoughts that arrive between the hours of 11pm and 7am. During those hours my brain is in lizard mode and thoughts that pop into my mind can take on a life of their own, snowballing into perilous worries or rumination in the darkness. So I remind myself of my 11–7 rule and set them aside.'

Underminers

A common thread between the saboteurs that we've considered so far is that they are about *us* – whether that be the voice of our inner critic, the importance we attach to what others think of us, the way that we can fall into traps of mindreading or overthinking, what we tell ourselves about perfection and failure or the risk of allowing tiredness to sap our confidence. It's true that in exploring what undermines our confidence, our focus is largely on how we sabotage ourselves. But we can't close this chapter without considering the way in which other people can sabotage our confidence.

We operate within a human system at work, a network of colleagues, suppliers, clients, partners, investors. Confidence can come and go depending on the level of nurture (or toxicity) within the human system in which we find ourselves. An environment with a healthy balance of honesty, support, challenge and respect can be a breeding ground for confidence. It's safe to try things out, mistakes are encouraged rather than shamed and progress is applauded. And the converse is true; our confidence can be sapped if we find ourselves in an environment that doesn't feel psychologically safe.

When I met coaching client Ria, her confidence was at a low ebb. She described a slow, steady diminishing of her self-belief as the result of a very difficult relationship with her manager, Georgina. Ria was allowed very little room to operate and was undermined by a constant (subtle) stream of criticism offered in the guise of support and coaching. As a result, Ria was paying the self-doubt tax in missed opportunities and unfulfilled potential. She had begun to question her capability and to second guess every decision that she made. Her diminishing confidence also had an impact outside of work as she struggled to step forward in social situations, despite historically being an outgoing and sociable individual. It was as though Ria had shrunk. As we worked together and I began to understand more about the dynamic between Ria and Georgina, it seemed to me that Georgina's overbearing leadership style was the result of a deep insecurity, which led her to search for control and to compete with others. I'm convinced that this was subconscious for Georgina – she did not get up in a morning and make a deliberate decision to belittle others – but that was the reality of her impact on Ria.

It took time for Ria to gradually rebuild her confidence, and Ria acknowledges that she didn't fully reclaim herself until she moved away from Georgina by changing role. There were two things that contributed to Ria's rebuilding of her confidence: perspective and support. Perspective was about supporting her to step outside of her situation and to take a look at it from a 'fly on the wall' position from which she could see the insecurity that drove Georgina's behaviour. Whilst this knowledge didn't immediately lessen the pain of a difficult interaction, over time it made the experience easier to withstand and enabled Ria to better calibrate

Georgina's harsh feedback and form her own evaluation of her contribution. She could separate out what was 'her stuff' and what was Georgina's. In addition, Ria confided in a close colleague and support from this individual was the second thing that contributed to Ria's renewed confidence. Her colleague offered a safe space to make sense of what she was going through and an alternative narrative that was encouraging, positive and focused on Ria's strengths.

Ria's story illustrates the way that our confidence can be intertwined with the words and actions of other people in ways that sap confidence and ways that boost confidence. Georgina's leadership style significantly weakened Ria's confidence and part of what helped Ria to rebuild was the support and encouragement of her colleague. We'll explore this intertwining in more depth in Chapter 7.

To sum up...

- All too often we unintentionally diminish our own confidence. By increasing our awareness of the confidence saboteurs in our own minds, we can keep them at bay.

- The thinking of our fear-driven inner critic is flawed. Knowing this and using a simple truth telling tool can help us to avoid falling prey to an inner critic hijack or believing the narrative that someone else is better than us.

- We're wired to care about what others think of us, but when that care tips over into fear, confidence can be dented. At the end of the day, there's one opinion of you that matters more than the others: yours.

- The trap of mindreading can be sidestepped if you swap the imaginings in your head for data. Ask what they are thinking.

- The antidote to the mental treadmill of overthinking is to bring your focus to the present moment.

- Perfectionism is an oppressor and good-enough-ism is a liberator, at the conceptual level of what it means to be a good enough human and at the practical level of what good enough looks like for a specific piece of work.

- It's an unavoidable truth that we all screw-up; mistakes and failure are part of life. Talking about failure can help us to increase our tolerance for the experience of things not going our way. And the bottom line is that we can survive failure; we can learn.

- A tired brain can't be rational. We need rest in order to reset and regain perspective.

- Our confidence is often intertwined with the words and actions of other people, and sometimes others can (deliberately or otherwise) undermine our self-belief.

6

Comings and goings

Our sense of confidence, the extent to which we trust ourselves, ebbs and flows over time. You might notice that the second year in a role brings a greater sense of ease than you experienced during the first year. You might know that your confidence changed when you had a child, changed career, got promoted, lost a parent, experienced a health issue. And it's not only across time that our confidence can vary, but also in different domains. Perhaps you're relaxed with your team, but distracted by your inner critic when meeting with peers? Perhaps you're comfortable to try a new hobby, but reluctant to stretch into different territory at work?

My invitation to you as you read this chapter is to reflect on the variations in your confidence, both over time and in different settings. In what ways does your confidence come and go? Reflecting on the ups and downs of your confidence provides insight that helps you to amplify the uplifts and lessen the dips.

A wobbly line

If I were to plot my confidence over time on a line graph, it wouldn't be a neat straight line. I think it would look a bit like a graph of the value of the FTSE 100 over my lifetime; the overall trend is upwards, but it's really scratchy in places. There are some big gains, a few big drops and a lot of little ups and downs, the accumulation of which is a significantly higher level of confidence now than the level I enjoyed 10, 20, 30 years ago.

If my imaginary line graph was the accepted way to map our confidence journeys – the way to accurately represent the way that our levels of confidence have varied over time – I suspect that the resulting graphs would be as unique as our fingerprints. Our backgrounds are different, we've faced our own blend of challenges and opportunities. Our personalities are different, what matters to us varies, and we've made our own set of life choices that have brought us to where we are right now. The chatter inside our head has a set of messages, a tone and a volume level that is unique to us. Our line graph would be unique, but I suspect that there's something universal about ups and downs. The wobbly line would be different, but it would be wobbly. Wobbles might be big or small, frequent or infrequent, but they would be there.

Kate Richardson-Walsh, captain of the gold medal winning women's hockey team at the Rio Olympics, reflected on her own wobbly line of confidence when she spoke to me for this book: 'I definitely had peaks and troughs. I had times when I felt I had reached a bit of mastery, but there were many times the whole way through my career where that dipped and waned. And I would really overthink every mistake I made. I would be stuck in a rut, I couldn't get myself out of it, and every mistake sent me deeper into that hole.'

Rebecca Snow, Global HR Vice President for Mars Snacking, highlighted a reason for a wobbly confidence line in a business setting. Zooming out and taking a perspective on her whole career, Rebecca could see that she has become significantly more confident over time, and she could see the stark differences in terms of scale and complexity between her first management role and her current global leadership role. In our conversation, Rebecca and I reflected on a relationship between the demands of the role, capability and confidence. Ideally, these three aspects would increase concurrently, so that as you step into a bigger job, the required competence came along with the move and you could immediately feel confident in your ability to meet the new demands. In reality, the job move often comes first – you step into a role that you're not fully ready for and then feel a degree of discomfort (and corresponding confidence dip) during the consciously incompetent stage. Later we'll explore the impact that job changes can have on our levels of confidence in more depth.

COACH YOURSELF CONFIDENT #27

 ## REFLECTION: Plot your confidence line graph

Draw the axes for a simple line graph on a piece of paper. The vertical axis represents your level of confidence and the horizontal axis represents time.

Now consider the time period that you'd like to plot. I'd recommend that it's a number of years. What you'll capture is a sense of.the ups and downs and the overall trend, not a scientifically detailed record. It might make sense to go back to the date that you started in your current organization, or even back to the beginning of your career.

Have a go at creating your confidence line graph. You might find it helpful to make some brief notes of dates / roles / events on a separate piece of paper first.

Add a few labels for any significant ups and downs, and then capture some brief notes on your reflections from creating the graph. You might think about:

- What's the overall trend over the period of time you have considered? Has your confidence increased or diminished?
- Which confidence saboteurs seem to be at play?
- What has contributed to the 'ups'? Are there any themes to draw out about what helps to build your confidence?

That so this

In response to a LinkedIn post in which I had set out a range of ways to complete the sentence 'Confidence is…', Evelyn Van Orden responded: 'At 67 years old, I'm finally feeling every aspect of confidence in your list. I earned every one of them through hard work and hard times. And I'm experiencing a feeling of inner peace that I've never felt before.' Evelyn's idea of 'earning confidence through hard work and hard times' is striking. Earning implies active effort; it's not simply a case of waiting for confidence to grow as we gain age and life experience. It's not automatic that the line on a confidence chart has an upward trajectory across time. But we can *earn* increased confidence; we can use the opportunities that life offers us to deepen our own understanding of what we're capable of. We can take encouragement from our ability to face difficulty and carry that encouragement with us to the next challenge.

In her book, *Why Has Nobody Told Me This Before?*, clinical psychologist Dr Julie Smith writes: 'Confidence is like a home that you build for yourself. When you go somewhere new, you must build a new one. But when we do, we're not starting from scratch. Every time we step into the unknown and try something new, experience that vulnerability, make mistakes, get through them and build some confidence, we move on to the next chapter with evidence that we can get through tough challenges. We bring with us the courage we need to take that leap of faith again and again.' What Dr Smith is eloquently describing is a process of building confidence based on experience, noticing evidence of our own capabilities and taking that evidence with us to our next challenge. It's the mindset of 'I have done that, so I can do this' that underpins our Confidence Momentum Cycle.

What's particularly powerful about the 'that so this' mindset is that it can generate homegrown confidence; a confidence that comes from within. A less potent confidence boost from the achievement of a task would be the belief that I can do that specific task again. I have done x, so I believe that I can do x again. The 'that so this' equation is different; I have done x, and that achievement fuels my belief that I can tackle y. In this way, achievement of x is strengthening your self-trust and extending your sense of what you are capable of. 'That so this' means building an internal inventory of your achievements and using that inventory as a springboard to do new things. The springboard allows you to jump into the unknown, with the confidence that you will land safely, even if you don't quite stick the landing perfectly every time.

There's an important point to emphasize here. When I talk about an inventory of your achievements, I'm thinking of a very broad definition of the word achievement. An achievement does not have to be completion of a big project or winning an award. An achievement is taking a step forward on a difficult task. An achievement is trying something new, even if it doesn't go entirely as planned. If we can applaud our willingness to take action, and take a clear-sighted view of our achievements, large and small, it helps us to build a line of confidence that has an upward trend. Confidence grows as we become more aware of our capabilities, as we see more clearly what we bring and what that enables, and expand the boundaries of our self-trust.

Sometimes the toughest of times prompt us to revise our self-view in a way that sharply increases our confidence. We experience an *if I can get through that, I can get through anything* moment. Being faced with a particularly gnarly problem, a thorny situation or an unexpected challenge can force us to find resources that we didn't know we had. We get through it, and we come out the other side fundamentally OK, surprised by what we were able to navigate. We didn't necessarily smash it, we might not be celebrating success, but we got through it. We faced something that we didn't know we could face. We dealt with it, we survived, and as a result, we reappraise ourselves. We can view our capabilities in a new way, perhaps with a new level of appreciation.

27th May 2004 was a strange day for me. It was the wedding day that didn't happen. The plans had been made, the venue booked, the dress ordered. But underneath the wedding planning excitement, I couldn't shake the gnawing feeling that things weren't right. With just over five months to go, I told my fiancé that I wanted to end our relationship. It was the hardest thing I had done in my life to that point. My fiancé was kind, he was a good man. There had been no fights, no dramatic rupture. We had a house together and our lives were interconnected in many ways. Making the break was painful, both emotionally and practically.

That was my *if I can get through that, I can get through anything* experience. I'm not sure how, but I mustered the strength to leave the relationship, and I leant on my family and friends to support me through the difficult time that followed. Before that experience, I wouldn't have thought myself able to risk disappointing others in such a significant way. I wouldn't have thought myself able to contemplate a 'failed' engagement, as someone who struggles with failure. But once I had done it, I was forced to reconsider my view of myself and to contemplate the possibility that I had underestimated what I was able to do, what I could withstand. This reappraisal of myself transcended domains. I had surprised myself in my personal life, so there was no reason why I couldn't surprise myself in a work setting too. What else might I be capable of? In this way, it was a liberating experience. I acknowledged that I didn't know the bounds of my capabilities, and I saw that my confidence level was not fixed.

I've observed this kind of reappraisal in others too. Jocelyne, a newly appointed manufacturing director was beginning to establish herself in role when a fire ripped through her biggest manufacturing facility. Thankfully, no one was seriously hurt, but the shock waves for the business were significant. Jocelyne and her team were plunged into crisis mode and their efforts were in the spotlight. They managed to re-establish supply within seven days, keeping their commercial colleagues informed throughout. It wasn't the start that Jocelyne had anticipated; it wasn't an event she would have wished for, but in hindsight, she could see how the experience helped her to settle into the big job. 'My leadership was tested in the very early days. It's the phone call no manufacturing leader wants to get. I felt sick. But I got through it. And knowing that I got through it gave me a boost in confidence. I started to really believe that I could be successful at this level.'

COACH YOURSELF CONFIDENT #28

 PRACTICE: Your 'that so this' inventory

Step 1

I invite you to create two versions of a 'that so this' inventory: one looking back over a long time frame and the other looking at the last six months. Take your time and capture as many items as you can in each list.

A long time frame	A short time frame
Think back over the years to times that you have surprised yourself – your *if I can get through that I can get through anything* moments.	Think back over the past six months and list as many achievements as you can think of – big and small.

Step 2

Now try bringing to mind something that you're facing, something that might be provoking a degree of self-doubt. Consider for a moment what it is that's triggering the self-doubt and then read through both of your inventories. What could you point to as evidence to suggest that you will be able to tackle the upcoming task / situation?

Steep drops

'You spend years building up confidence and then it disappears in a puff of smoke.' These were the words of a client as she described her experience of an exceptionally high pressure situation during an acquisition process. As the person leading the attempt to acquire a sizeable competitor business, Tessa's focus was divided between the acquisition team of colleagues and external advisors, her peers on the country leadership team and the global executive board. And she still had responsibility for the day-to-day running of her business unit. It's no wonder that she was feeling intellectually stretched and physically exhausted from regular 16- to 18-hour days.

The 'puff of smoke' moment came in an update to the global executive team; the result of a terse exchange and the evident frustration of the global CEO who couldn't understand why progress wasn't being made faster. To Tessa, the unspoken message seemed clear: *Your approach isn't good enough. You're not good enough.* Her confidence evaporated and she began to pay a high self-doubt tax. She battled with a harsh inner critic voice that had completely absorbed the criticism of the CEO, she felt anxious for much of the time, and she struggled to sleep. When she approached me for coaching support, Tessa could see that she was in a downward spiral. Feeling an enormous sense of responsibility and being understandably exhausted, her psychological defences were low. Her inner critic was on high alert. She was deeply wounded by any (real or imagined) criticism, she heard requests as disappointment, and she struggled to hold boundaries.

As I look back at our work together, there were two core elements that helped Tessa to rebuild her confidence. The first was support. Whilst she had strong relationships inside and outside the organization, Tessa was not used to asking for support. More often she was the person who others turned to for help, and she took pride in a degree of self-sufficiency. The coaching helped Tessa to realize that making use of this previously untapped well of support could help her to withstand the pressure she was under. She identified two trusted colleagues and began opening up about her experience of the acquisition process. In Tessa's words, this was 'settling' and helped her to 'put things in perspective'. Hearing that a colleague had also been bruised by an experience with the global CEO provided a degree of reassurance. Tessa began to form a more rounded narrative about her experience: perhaps the difficult interaction with the CEO was not only about Tessa's 'inadequacies', but also about the CEO's response to pressure. The second element that helped was an exercise in which I invited Tessa to mentally travel forward in time, an exercise designed to gain a different perspective on her current challenges. This enabled Tessa to see the situation for what it was: a difficult episode in a much longer story, rather than a moment that defined who she was or what she could do.

Bumps and knocks

Drops in confidence are not always as dramatic as was the case in Tessa's story, but I think that dips are inevitable. Plans will go awry, hiccups will happen, mistakes will be made. Bumps and knocks are unavoidable, and in the face of the inevitable surprises, obstacles and errors, we can feel our confidence dip. Our inner critic pipes up with a commentary that makes it very personal: *You should have anticipated that. How did you let that slip, you idiot? It's never going to work now. Everyone has lost faith in you.* And so on. Inner critics can really get on a roll sometimes. If we're not careful, we can get stuck in the setback loop of our Confidence Momentum Cycle, unable to find a way to move forward and take action again.

As I carried out the research for this book, I heard a consistent theme. Setbacks might be difficult at the time, but the process of overcoming those setbacks contributes to a growing level of self-trust. 'In the difficult moments, when I feel small, I remember how far I have come and that I have conquered every challenge.' 'It wasn't necessarily the most enjoyable time – everything seemed to go wrong – but I undoubtedly grew from the experience. I was a more confident person at the end of those six months.' Fellow coach Andy Brett put it beautifully: 'Confidence is the quiet, steady feeling of "I've got this" that (for me) comes with the knowledge that I've screwed-up in pretty much every way possible at some point in the past and recovered each time.' Acknowledging that you've had setbacks and you've overcome them is another version of 'that so this': *I messed up a, b, c, d, e, f… and I'm still OK, so I can take on whatever comes next.*

Martin Seligman, psychologist and author of *Learned Optimism: How to Change your Mind and Your Life*, suggests a simple way to frame setbacks that helps us to keep them in perspective. Seligman identified that the way we talk to ourselves about a setback makes a significant difference to how we feel about it and to our capacity to maintain momentum. If our internal narrative is pessimistic, we characterize the setback as *permanent, pervasive* and *personal.* Your proposal doesn't get approved and you think: *I'm never going to be able to move this forward, it's too hard to get things done here,*

I did a terrible job of my presentation. Perhaps unsurprisingly, Seligman found that talking to ourselves in this way can be debilitating. It can diminish performance, trigger depression and 'turn setbacks into disasters'.[31]

The three Ps – permanent, pervasive and personal – serve to exaggerate the significance of the setback. Rather than looking for learnings and correcting our course, we come to a halt. It's hard to take action because we've lost faith in ourselves. The alternative to the three Ps is characterizing the setback as *temporary, specific* and *external.* With this narrative, we're more likely to persist when things don't work out as we'd expected. We can look for the learnings and try again. The reaction to our proposal being turned down becomes: *It didn't go my way today, this idea will need a bit more work, the steering committee might need more time.*

COACH YOURSELF CONFIDENT #29

 PRACTICE: Putting a setback in perspective

Next time you experience a setback, take a few minutes to notice your reaction and write down your thoughts. Now do a bit of P-spotting – are you characterizing the setback as permanent, pervasive and / or personal?

---

[31] Seligman, 2006 cited in Pink, 2014.

158 Coach Yourself Confident

If you see signs of any of the three Ps, then you might need to do a bit of work to shrink the setback down to size in your mind. You do this by finding a different way to characterize it, so it no longer seems permanent, pervasive or personal, but is instead temporary, specific and external.

Consider asking a supportive colleague to talk it through with you, helping you to edit out the three Ps and put the setback into perspective.

Job changes

A new job can be an invitation for self-doubt and what-ifs. Perhaps you've mustered all of your confidence to talk yourself up in an interview. You've spoken with a level of conviction that you don't really feel. You've convinced the hiring manager that you're the best candidate for the role and now it's time to begin work. *What if I can't do it? What if I mess it up? What if I've convinced them that I'm better than I am? What if I disappoint them? What if I disappoint myself? What if I don't like the role? What if this was a bad decision?*

If you recognize that you're someone whose confidence lags behind your capability, then applying for a new job probably means that you do quite a lot of pretending. You take on the role of a confident, capable candidate for the duration of the process. It's not easy, but you force yourself to do it, preparing for the selection process and then portraying the most confident version of yourself. You find a way to voice your strengths and own your accomplishments, knowing that this is what's required in the process. Unfortunately, as you listen to yourself describe this capable and accomplished person, you don't really believe the story that you are telling. You know that you're doing what's required as a candidate for a job, but you can't help feeling a little fraudulent. You're talking yourself up and presenting a version of yourself that you don't quite recognize. You're hoping that you can fool the decision makers, but you don't succeed in fooling yourself.

The job offer comes and an initial feeling of elation might rapidly give way to a worry about whether you've done the right thing. Perhaps you've oversold yourself. Perhaps you've taken too much of a risk. Perhaps you should have stayed within the safety of the role that you know. The impending reality of stepping into the new role is like pressing a self doubt reset button. You only managed to quieten your self-doubt for the length of the application process, and as soon as you get the job, your harsh inner critic reappears and is determined to make up for lost time.

One response to a brash inner critic in the lead up to a new role is to go all out to prove them wrong. You decide that you'll smash it. And in doing so, you set yourself up for disappointment. This sort of determination to prove yourself from day one, to step into the new role seamlessly and to immediately fulfil – or even exceed – expectations sets up an unreachable bar. It comes from a place of self-doubt, a place of fear. *I'm either brilliant from day one or I'm not good enough. I make an impressive impact or they will see that they have made a mistake.* This unrealistic expectation of yourself doesn't allow for learning. It doesn't allow for the reality that there are differences between your old job and your new job, and that those differences are gaps in knowledge and skill that need to be bridged by learning. Setting a 'brilliant from day one' expectation hands power to your inner critic, allowing them to characterize the inevitable gaps in knowledge and skill as deficits in you. Instead of seeing that you don't know how to do something because this new job is a stretch, your internal narrative is diminishing: *I don't know how to do that, but I should*. And your internal narrative is full of threat: *They will see that they've made mistake, that I'm not up to it*.

Day one doesn't have to be in a new job to bring with it the risk of a painful dip in confidence. Returning from maternity leave can trigger an attack of self-doubt, even for those who see themselves as having a good level of confidence. A coaching client, Niamh told me: 'I didn't think that I'd feel wobbly about coming back. I love my job and I'm good at it. But six months is a long time in this organization. Will my supporters remember what I can do? Will they still advocate for me?'

As well as this kind of concern about our reputation and sponsorship, many maternity returners face an enforced change to their mode of operating with a new childcare routine to adapt to. For self-doubt taxpayers who previously substituted hard work and extra hours for an inner sense of confidence, this is particularly challenging. They cannot compensate for their self-doubt in the same way because additional hours aren't available to them now that they need to leave to collect their child at the end of the day. Over-workers often draw their confidence from their achievements. It's their track record of delivery that they look towards in order to convince themselves (and others) of their capability. At the point of stepping back into the business post-maternity leave, there's a hiatus in their history of work achievements. There's x months during which there are no deliverables to point to. It feels like starting again, like day one in a new business, and the inner critic ratchets up the pressure to prove.

Of course, this painful return experience is not universal. Some maternity returners step back into the business with a large dose of *if I got through that I can get through anything*. Or they bring with them a fundamental shift in perspective which enables them to loosen their grip on being brilliant at work. They accept the new constraints within which they need to work and reshape their contribution. I've worked alongside numerous maternity returners whose productivity and focus has sharpened. They simply get more done in fewer hours. And the boundary represented by a new family role enables them to say no and to manage expectations in a way that had previously felt uncomfortable.

Careers can take unexpected turns and job changes are sometimes thrust upon us uninvited in the form of redundancy or restructure. Such events can trigger a steep decline in confidence. Redundancy and restructure are both about roles rather than individuals, but of course it feels personal. It's all too easy to translate *I wasn't selected for a role in the new structure* to *I'm no good at what I do* to *I'm a failure*. There aren't many people who wouldn't find their confidence dinted by the shock of this kind of unexpected job change. The risk is that we build a catastrophizing narrative on top of the thought that *I'm a failure… I won't get another job. I won't be able to pay the rent / mortgage. My partner will leave me…* What's particularly difficult is that it is in this moment that we most need our confidence. We need to find a new role, and that means putting ourselves out there, applying for jobs and portraying the most confident version of ourselves.

I'm not generally a fan of the 'fake it 'til you make it' school of confidence building, but in my view it's the right approach in this situation. Pretend away. The primary goal is to enable a hiring manager to see your true capabilities, even if you can't fully see them yourself. Usefully, it's possible to use the process of applying for roles as a way to build your confidence – that's what the next *Coach Yourself Confident* practice is about.

COACH YOURSELF CONFIDENT #30

 PRACTICE: Use your job application as a confidence builder

Writing your CV and preparing for interviews can be an exercise in cataloguing your achievements, building your 'that so this' data. You are collating evidence to support your application: *If I did all of these things, I can do this role*. Enlist a friend to help you, someone who can call you out when you're underplaying your track record.

You could also ask your friend to play back your achievements to you in a way that is untinged by self-doubt. This is an interesting exercise in itself – listening to your achievements being played back to you. Really listen and try to absorb what you hear. This is a version of your achievements that is free from amusement arcade mirror distortions. Make notes to read and re-read. The more you can learn to recognize this undistorted version of your own track record, the more you will trust in yourself.

When you've secured your next role, put all of those notes somewhere safe and return to them when you've begun to settle in. At this point, you might be more able to absorb the undistorted narrative, to take ownership for your achievements and your strengths.

Free range confidence

'We overlook the primordial need to acquire a more free-ranging variety of confidence – one that can serve us across a range of tasks: speaking to strangers at parties, asking someone to marry us, suggesting a fellow passenger turn down their music, changing the world.'[32] I love this extract from The School of Life's collection of essays *On Confidence*. The point is beautifully made that confidence is situational. Your feeling of confidence might vary:

- in different aspects of your role.
- within the organization, outside the organization.
- with this team, with another team.
- with this client, with another client.
- when taking on a new responsibility.
- when dealing with a crisis.

---

[32] *The School of Life. On Confidence.* 2017.

- as you engage in your hobbies.
- when you're with friends.
- in social settings, big and small.
- when dealing with a home emergency.

I'm in my element on stage in front of 400 strangers, but I can feel really uncomfortable in a social setting where I don't know people well. I think perhaps this is because in the social setting, there's no expertise to hide behind, and no way of doing preparation to reassure myself. I'm 'just me' rather than Julie Smith, exec coach. This tells me something about where I draw my confidence from. It comes (in part) from knowing what I'm doing, from my expertise. I know that I can stand on stage and hold the audience's attention on a topic in my sphere. I'm far less certain that I can hold the attention of someone I've just met at a party.

For two decades, Sarah Dickens performed as a professional dancer and singer. Her career took her all around the world before she achieved her dream of performing in London's West End, enjoying success in hit musicals such as *Starlight Express* and *Fame*. When a serious knee problem forced her to give up stage roles, Sarah initially stayed within the world of theatre in a behind the scenes role, but ultimately the theatre stairs proved too much for Sarah's knees and she was forced to find work outside of show business. At the age of 43, Sarah looked for her first ever non-theatre job and became a receptionist.

The private equity firm in which she found herself felt like a foreign land for Sarah and the experience was deeply disorienting. Having been confident in her identity as a dancer and at ease on the stage, Sarah felt adrift in this new domain.

For many of us, being behind a reception desk might seem significantly less nerve-wracking than performing on stage, but for Sarah, finding herself in such unknown territory triggered a sharp dip in confidence. 'What am I doing here? I don't know how to do anything in this setting.' Just because Sarah appeared supremely confident on stage, belting out *Fame* and making that iconic split jump from the top of the yellow taxicab didn't mean that she could easily access her confidence in a completely different setting. In her office job, Sarah felt like an imposter. It took a few years and a move into teaching for Sarah to fully recover her work confidence.

I heard a similar theme in other interviews. Kate Richardson-Walsh found the transition into a corporate role 'hideous' after she retired as a professional hockey player. BBC weather presenter Chris Fawkes (who broadcasts to millions in his work) confessed to nerves when he arrived at a school expecting to talk to a class and found that he was being asked to speak in front of an entire year group. All of these stories illustrate that confidence can be domain specific.

I suggest that it's helpful to hold our humble confidence mantra in mind as we step into a new domain: *I am good enough and I can be better.* The mantra acknowledges two fundamental truths. Firstly, that your self-worth is not attached to your performance in this new domain – you are *good enough* simply because of who you are. Secondly, that you have the capacity to grow and develop. By definition, a beginner has scope to learn. This is not a deficiency, it's simply the reality; when you start something new, you're not immediately skilled and at ease, but you can grow your skill (and your sense of ease) through focus and practice. You're not good at this new thing *yet*, but you will improve in time.

To sum up...

- Confidence comes and goes. A graphical representation of our confidence over a number of years would look pretty wobbly. Even if the overall trend is upwards, the confidence line will have many ups and downs.

- Looking back can fuel our confidence, with a 'that so this' inventory reminding us of what we've achieved.

- Sometimes we might surprise ourselves with an ability to find our way through a tricky situation. If we use this as a trigger to recalibrate our sense of self, then we can expand our understanding of what we're capable of and fuel our confidence with the idea that *if I can get through that, I can get through anything.*

- Techniques to gain a balanced perspective can help us to navigate experiences that knock our confidence. Mental time travel can remind us that a steep drop in confidence is situational, not a permanent reset. Framing setbacks as temporary, specific and external can help to shrink a setback down to size in our mind.

- A new job can be an invitation for self-doubt and what-ifs, something that can be turned on its head by consciously using the job application process as a 'that so this' confidence boost.

- Confidence is situational – our self-assurance in a particular domain doesn't necessarily transfer to a different setting. The humble confidence mantra reminds us that our self-worth is not dependent on how we perform and that we have an endless capacity to learn.

7

Homegrown confidence

The most robust version of confidence is grown from within. You could think of it as a plant that you nurture by providing the water and food required to nourish and sustain it. There is a solidity to this homegrown confidence, a solidity that brings to mind Maya Angelou's words: 'Nothing can dim the light which shines from within.' This robust, internally generated feeling of confidence enables you to withstand the inevitable bumps and knocks. Imagine receiving a poor appraisal rating or having an important business proposal turned down. It might be disappointing or frustrating, or even make you angry. But it doesn't fundamentally change your view of yourself and what you're capable of. You can look for the lessons to be learned without that being in any way diminishing. You can look for the 'so what' rather than allowing your inner critic to take charge of a search for all of the reasons why you are a failure.

Of course, boosts to your confidence often spring from external sources: a job title that provides a label for your level of achievement, qualifications that signpost your knowledge or the praise that you receive from others. These boosts can make a difference to the way that you feel about yourself, triggering pride and swelling your confidence. But there's a risk of this being a temporary impact. If you don't internalize these reasons to be confident, if you don't use them as a catalyst to update your self-image and reappraise your sense of your own capability, then the lift in confidence is fleeting.

Our focus in this final chapter is on the kind of homegrown confidence that shines brightly from within. Instead of relying on external crutches for your confidence, you nurture your own realistic (and constantly evolving) sense of self. This is homegrown, humble confidence.

Confidence by proxy

Let's begin our exploration of homegrown confidence by looking at some ways in which we can station confidence outside of ourselves. I'll start with qualifications. Sometimes I see individuals who use qualifications as a confidence life raft. The qualification is seen as an objective measure of their capability (*See! This authority has validated me*). They can be confident because an awarding body has told them that they are allowed to be. A certificate is the thing that they can use to convince themselves that they know what they're doing. But this feeling of self-assurance can be fleeting. There's a fragility to self-belief that relies on qualifications. Unless the individual uses the qualification as a means to recalibrate their understanding of themselves and their capability, then the confidence boost gained from attaining the qualification can quickly fade. It's not enough, they need to go after the next qualification. There's a sense of striving, of searching for something that remains out of reach.

One way to internalize the confidence boost of a new qualification is to take the time to reflect on what you have gained from the process of completing the qualification, taking a really broad view on the question. How has the experience strengthened your skills? What are you taking away from the experience in addition to that hard-won certificate? Perhaps you have deepened your competence in critical thinking, articulating an argument, planning and organizing, speaking up.

For some, it's the label of a job title or grade that acts as the external proxy for internally felt confidence. I remember what my coaching client Anaya said about her promotion to a 'Head of' role, a significant transition into senior leadership in her organization. 'I feel like I can finally exhale. I felt a bit like I was pretending before, and I thought that everyone else could see that. It's totally changed my confidence.' On one level, this was something to be celebrated, a boost in confidence to be built on. The key question was whether this new felt confidence could be internalized, whether Anaya could use the promotion as a trigger to enhance a sense of humble confidence from within. I have seen multiple clients who have worked hard to progress, but then at the point of promotion have felt slightly fraudulent. They hold tight to the new job title, thankful for the validation that it offers, but don't yet feel as though it really fits them. They have been promoted by the organization, they have picked up their new responsibilities, but they haven't mentally promoted themselves.

COACH YOURSELF CONFIDENT #31

 PRACTICE: Promote yourself

A simple way to kick-start the mental process of promoting yourself is to write an announcement about your new role. This isn't an announcement that you'll share with anyone else – what you're really doing is announcing the promotion to yourself.

The intention is to clearly and fully articulate the reasons why the promotion is well deserved. You might consider the behaviours that you demonstrate, the values that you're known for, the feedback offered to you by colleagues, the outcomes that you have delivered, the changes you have made.

You're not aiming for an overblown press release; you're aiming for a clear and factual piece in which you articulate how you have earned this well-deserved step up.

Once you've written your announcement-to-self, read it carefully, perhaps out loud. See if you can really absorb the facts that you have set out.

Over-reliance on others

Whilst some people use qualifications or status as a confidence crutch, others rely on other people to prop up their confidence. There's a psychological underpinning to acknowledge here. William James, a giant in the history of psychology, stated in an 1896 letter to his students: 'The deepest principle in human nature is the craving to be appreciated.' As human beings, we want to be seen and valued by others. We are wired to care what people think of us, but when this care is overplayed we place too much emphasis on how others see us. We seek external validation in the form of praise and affirmation from others in order to feel good about ourselves. Caring too much about what people think of us leaves us reliant on others: we can only have self-trust if others trust in our skills and abilities.

Outsourcing our sense of self to others, being reliant on their approval and praise, is both natural and risky. We've all been children, and during early childhood our sense of OK-ness has come from our parents. It's not surprising that many of us take this experience into our adulthood, taking with us a belief that the source of OK-ness is 'out there' rather than 'in here'. We continue to look to others for reassurance, and we build our confidence based on the way that others evaluate our capabilities. In doing so, we are placing responsibility for our view of ourselves into the hands of others, looking for external validation because we can't or don't generate it for ourselves.

Ohio State University psychologist Jennifer Crocker has discovered that people who base their self-worth and self-confidence on what others think of them pay a physical price. Crocker's study of six hundred college students showed that those who depended on others for approval — of their appearance, grades, choices — reported more stress and had higher levels of drug abuse and eating disorders. The students who based their self-esteem and confidence on internal sources, such as being clear on their values and living in line with those values, did better than the others in exams and had lower levels of drug and alcohol abuse.[33]

Borrowing confidence

Playing the clarinet calms my mind and brings me joy. I'm a part-time musician, rehearsing once a week with my concert band and performing regularly. A few months back, as I arrived at rehearsal, I was intercepted by our chairperson, Ian, who asked if I'd step up to play second clarinet for that rehearsal and for the upcoming concert. And – this bit was important – he told me that he and the band's conductor, Dave, had decided that I was the person to ask. They didn't choose one of my fellow players on the third clarinet part, they chose me. Weirdly, my clarinet playing immediately improved. It was far from perfect, but I made a really good stab at the second clarinet part, even though I was seeing it for the first time. What was this magic, this immediate improvement in

[33] Kay and Shipman, 2014.

my musical skill? It was me believing someone else's view of my capability. *If they – who are proper musicians who know what they're talking about – think I can do it, then I must be able to.*

If we're relying on others for validation, then it builds our confidence when we hear positive things, but confidence can crash when they criticize. We have invested power in their opinion; good when the opinion is a positive one, potentially disastrously undermining when it isn't. Our sense of our own ability is based on what they think. Our sense of self is only on loan to us and our confidence is only present for as long as the other person holds a positive evaluation of us. If that person is our boss and they change jobs, our confidence evaporates. If the cheerleaders from whom we borrow our confidence are within the organization where we work, what does that mean for our ability to choose to leave? Can we really risk leaving our sense of confidence behind, in the hands of our former colleagues?

As we saw when we explored comparisonitis in Chapter 5, organization hierarchy invites an assumption that more senior equals more knowledgeable, more insightfulness, better, and it can be tempting to borrow our confidence from these 'better' colleagues. 'When someone senior trusts me, I can be more confident. I can take a bit more risk, take the initiative rather than shrinking.' Janaav recognized that encouraging messages from senior colleagues had a high impact on his confidence, and then in turn on his willingness to act, to drive the business forward. He could feel confident as a result of the validation from an authority figure, someone at a higher grade. Working together, we explored how Janaav might develop a practice of providing the encouragement for himself. How can he extend to himself the same level of respect that he extends to those who are above him in the organizational hierarchy? How can he gradually shift the locus of his confidence from outside of himself to within himself? This involved supporting him to own his strengths and achievements, using tools like the Coach Yourself Confident #12 reflection: *I am good enough.*

People pleasing

If we're reliant on others for our confidence, for our sense of self, then it follows that we're likely to do whatever we can to ensure that those others hold a positive view of us. One of the ways that we might do that is to focus on pleasing. Pleasing people is not in itself a bad thing; it's wonderful to demonstrate kindness and consideration, to help someone out. The issue is when the driver behind such actions is about seeking (or maintaining) the approval of others. When this driver is at play, pleasing others is a compulsion rather than a choice, and we find it immensely difficult to displease or disappoint those around us. Do you sometimes find yourself saying yes when you want to say no? Do you sometimes put the needs of others ahead of your own? Caring about people's opinions needs to include caring about your own opinion, your own needs. What do *you* think? How do *you* feel? What do *you* want?

There will be times when what you want and need clashes with what is being asked of you by someone else. Increasing your ability to displease others means noticing these clashes and choosing to say no to the request that's being made of you. 'Disappoint people with regret, but do disappoint them,' wrote Sonia March Nevis, a key figure in the field of Gestalt therapy. I'm reminded of a scene from the classic sitcom Friends when Joey asks Phoebe to help put together Ross's new furniture. Phoebe's reply: 'I wish I could... but I don't want to.' Perhaps a few of us could do with an inner Phoebe to help us to clean up our yes and no responses to things, to help us to say yes only when we want to do so, not out of a sense of duty or obligation. This might feel like a big shift to make, so let me offer you a place to start: learn to say no by delaying the yes. Start small by interrupting the automatic yes response and giving yourself time to think about it. By giving yourself time, you'll be able to decide if it is something you have the desire and time to take on.

COACH YOURSELF CONFIDENT #32

 PRACTICE: From fearing to caring

This practice is about a recalibration of your relationship to the opinions of others. It's about a shift away from external validation and towards internal validation. A move from *fearing* other people's opinions to *caring* about other people's opinions. It's about putting a boundary around what William James called 'the craving to be appreciated' and ensuring that the craving does not get out of control.

What does such a recalibration look like? Let me try to sketch out the difference by means of a few examples. As you read through them, notice if any of the examples resonate with you.

FOPO (Fear of people's opinions)	CAPO (Care about people's opinions)
Saying yes out of obligation or out of fear that saying no will lead others to think badly of me.	Fully understanding the request and why it is being made, and then saying yes on the basis of a calm assessment of my own capacity, capability and motivation.
Dwelling on a negative comment that someone makes about a project I delivered.	Seeing the comment as data about the project, data which may or may not be useful. Considering it as objectively as possible and comparing it to my own perspective.
Censoring myself, shaping what I say based on how I think it will land with others.	Saying what I think clearly and straightforwardly. Being open to developing that thinking through adult-to-adult discussion with others.
Pretending to agree with others even though I feel differently.	Speaking up when I have a different point of view, showing respect for my own point of view and that of others.
Apologizing / taking the blame even when something isn't my fault.	Taking responsibility for my own actions and apologizing when needed. Holding others to account for their behaviour.

Leaving ourselves vulnerable

Stationing our confidence outside of ourselves and relying on others for our sense of self leaves us vulnerable. 'When I'm with Mike, I just overthink. I second guess everything and I try to tell him what he wants to hear.' These were the words of Scott, a coaching client who was grappling with a new leadership role within a fast-moving organization. Mike was his boss, the ambitious and razor sharp CEO whose leadership style was one of high challenge. A highly driven self-starter with rock solid self-belief, Mike didn't look to others for validation, and it didn't occur to him that his team might need praise or reassurance. In his words, 'the fact that they still have a job tells them everything they need to know – they wouldn't still be here if I didn't think they were delivering.'

Scott found his relationship with Mike deeply uncomfortable. Scott's inner critic was brutal, and he looked to others to balance the harshness of this internal narrative. He needed others, particularly his boss, to reassure him that he was good enough, that he was making the right calls and having an impact. Reassurance was not what Scott heard from Mike. Instead, he heard Mike ask for more and more. Each success that Scott delivered triggered more questions, more challenges, more to do. In Scott's mind, the message was clear: *You're failing*. After a while, every interaction with Mike served to further drain Scott's confidence as he interpreted almost anything his boss said as an indication of a lack of faith in him. Scott's brain would become foggy, making clear thinking difficult and further diminishing his self-belief.

I need to be clear here. Yes, Mike's leadership style might be experienced by many as tough, demanding, even a little cold. But it's not as simple as saying that Mike sabotaged Scott's confidence. It was the combination of Mike's style with Scott's habit of outsourcing his confidence that drained his self-belief. Eleanor Roosevelt's quote is well known: 'No one can make you feel inferior without your consent.' Scott gave his consent. And he did so because of his own self-doubt. His one-to-ones with Mike were full of shit snap moments where his inner critic grabbed hold of something Mike said, twisted the words and then shouted *See – I told you so! He thinks you're useless at this job.* The irony was that in fact Mike believed that Scott was delivering brilliantly. The game of shit snap that he was playing was imaginary.

The work for Scott to do was two-fold. Firstly, I supported him to find ways to manage his state in the interactions with Mike, to lessen the mental panic that he felt and allow him to think more clearly. Secondly, the deeper and more challenging work was to look at his own self-doubt, to see that the villain here was not Mike, but his own inner critic. Scott needed to reflect on the reasons why he outsourced his confidence to others and to begin to build homegrown confidence. Without doing this work, we allow others direct access to our sense of self. The School of Life writers put it like this: 'The judgements of others have been given a free pass to enter all the rooms of our minds. There is no one manning the border between them and us: the enemies are freely in us, wandering wildly and destructively through the caverns of our inner selves, ripping items off the shelves and mocking everything we are.'[34]

---

[34] The School of Life. *On Confidence.* 2017.

COACH YOURSELF CONFIDENT #33

 PRACTICE: Test your interpretation

This practice is about noticing when we allow someone else to dent our confidence, then pressing pause and challenging our interpretation of the situation. It's a practice that I used in my work with Scott. If you can bring to mind a recent situation when you allowed someone to dent your confidence, you could test out this practice now.

Step 1: What happened

Note down what happened – what was it that triggered a dip in your confidence?

> *I called Elizabeth to update her on the current project issue and she was really short with me. Her answers were abrupt and she ended the call after only a few minutes.*

Step 2: Interpretations that are about me

Capture the assumptions that you are making. These are likely to be interpretations of the other person's words and actions that centre on you.

> *She thinks I'm useless at my job.*
>
> *She's disappointed with the way I delivered that project.*

She wants to get rid of me.

Step 3: Interpretations that are not about me

Now write down as many alternative interpretations as you can come up with – explanations for the other person's actions and words that don't centre on you.

She was distracted by something else – her shortness wasn't anything to do with me.

She's really feeling the pressure at the moment.

She's got something tricky going on at home.

She was in a hurry to get to another meeting.

Step 4: How I choose to respond

Now think about what you choose to do next.

I'll schedule a one-to-one for Elizabeth and me to review progress on the project, and I'll ask her directly for some feedback.

Confidence in community

Over the last few pages, we've explored the impact of relying on others for our confidence – basing our view of ourselves on what other people think. In my clarinet playing example, borrowing confidence served to improve my musical skill, a positive (if temporary) impact. But in the example of my coaching client, Scott, we saw just how risky borrowing confidence can be. Scott lacked a solid belief in himself and relied on the views of others to bolster his confidence. When reassurance and praise were not forthcoming, Scott experienced the pain of being unable to borrow confidence from Mike and being unable to generate his own.

From borrowed to owned

I want to look more closely at this idea of borrowing confidence because there is an important nuance to consider. It's not as straightforward as 'borrowing confidence = bad'. Borrowed confidence is OK if it's a short term loan, a sort of try-before-you-buy arrangement rather than a long-term lending library. For me, borrowing confidence from a supportive leader was a step on my journey to generating a more solid, internal belief in my own capability. In my twenties, I worked for an incredible and inspiring HR leader. Jackie was powerful, in the most positive sense of that word. She had vision, she had guts and she had compassion. Jackie became my line manager a few months after I joined PepsiCo, and I worked for her either directly or indirectly for the next decade. Over the course of those years, Jackie gave me a range of different opportunities, all stretching, some more enjoyable than others. She invited me to do things that I didn't feel ready for. She promoted me three times, including the step into my first role with the word director in the title. That felt like a big deal at the time, although in hindsight I can see that I was taking some confidence from the external validation of a job title.

Jackie believed in me so consistently and so wholeheartedly that I eventually had to believe in myself. I moved from borrowing my confidence from Jackie to owning it, from outsourcing my confidence to feeling it from within. I started to believe that I was good enough. Jackie was a believer, and I am eternally grateful to her for that. Believers can help us to find our confidence for ourselves, following the path that they set out through unstinting belief and encouragement. There's a broader point here too, a point about growing confidence in community. With support, it's easier to take action, easier to navigate setbacks, easier to pull out the learnings when things don't go to plan, easier to celebrate successes when they do.

The purpose of the next exercise is to consider the extent of your support network and the way that you make use of the support that's available to you.

COACH YOURSELF CONFIDENT #34

 REFLECTION: My support network

Step 1

Take a few minutes to map who is in your support network, using the categories offered below. These different supporter roles are based on the work of Zella King and Amanda Scott.[35]

---

[35] King and Scott, 2014.

Role	Who?
Cheerleader: someone who has faith in your abilities and offers heartfelt encouragement.	
Improver: someone who gives candid, constructive feedback on your performance and development.	
Challenger: someone who challenges your decisions and thinking.	
Nerve-giver: someone who strengthens your resolve at difficult times.	
Anchor: someone who keeps you grounded and holds you to account for the balance between your work and the rest of your life.	

Step 2

Now reflect on how well you make use of the support that's available to you. Is there more that you could do to tap into the support on offer?

Step 2 in the Coach Yourself Confident #34 (above) is important: a consideration of how well you make use of the support that's available to you. Our Supporters can only support us to the extent that we let them. In order to benefit from our Challengers, we need to seek out their different way of thinking. If a Nerve-giver is to strengthen our resolve, we need to tell them that we're wavering. And in order to own the confidence that our Cheerleaders offer to us (rather than borrowing it from them temporarily), we need to absorb what they tell us. We need to internalize their praise and allow the belief that they have in us to fuel our self-belief. I invite you to explore the extent to which you do this by working through the next *Coach Yourself Confident* reflection activity.

COACH YOURSELF CONFIDENT #35

 REFLECTION: (Really) hearing your cheerleaders

Pick one of your cheerleaders – someone who makes you feel good about yourself.

Use the scale below to reflect on the extent to which you absorb what they say.

⬅───────────────────────────➡

I keep it OUT   I allow it IN
I find reasons for doubt   I accept it as valid data

If you tend towards the 'keep it out' end of the scale, with thoughts such as *their default setting is positive, they don't really mean it*, here's a quick exercise to try.

Write a couple of paragraphs about yourself, using the voice of your biggest supporter. Try to capture what they would say, without in any way discounting their positive view.

Just enough support

You might imagine that what we need to seek out are the kind of people who will support us without question, who will provide reassurance when we need it, will pour water into our inner well of self-confidence. Yes and no. Too much support can be a wolf in sheep's clothing, giving us a warm feeling of reassurance, whilst quietly and steadily sapping our confidence. The process is more benign than Scott's experience with Mike, but the result is the same: a hit to confidence.

Maria Montessori was an Italian physician born in 1870. She developed a method of education based on her belief in a child's ability to reach their potential on their own if given the freedom and the environment to develop naturally. At Montessori schools, children are extended trust in order to build their independence and their confidence. 'Never help a child perform a task that he feels capable of accomplishing himself' was the mantra constantly repeated by the movement's founder. In other words, trust the student as soon as possible. The mantra is powerful because it conveys to the child that the teacher believes in them. It communicates 'I have confidence in you' with the aim of prompting the child to have confidence in themselves. Children are encouraged to find out what they are capable of; they are encouraged to trust themselves. Of course, this philosophy is not confined to Montessori schools. If you're a parent, you might recognize it in your own parenting or in the approach of your child's nursery or school.

The Montessori approach illustrates the power of offering *just enough* support – no more than is needed. If a teacher or caregiver steps in to assist a child to do something that they might be able to do on their own, this kind-hearted action risks interrupting the process of the child learning to trust themselves. Similarly, as adults, if we have colleagues who step forward with more support than we need, then their kind-hearted intentions are counterproductive. When a boss takes too much care of us, doesn't push us to add to our skills, steps in to save us from tricky moments with others, they are communicating a message that we need to be taken care of. We need to be looked after because we lack the ability to manage ourselves, to sit with the discomfort of disagreement, to find ways to expand our repertoire of skill. They communicate a lack of trust in us, which will in turn feed our lack of trust in ourselves; our lack of confidence.

I'm not saying that we need a boss who constantly pushes us to the edge of our comfort zone and beyond. That can be exhausting and can have a negative impact on our confidence, but neither do we want someone to take it upon themselves to keep us cocooned and comfortable. The risk here is that over time the comfort zone gets smaller as we rely on our boss to make the right decisions for us and doubt our own ability to do so. The *Coach Yourself Confident* reflection below offers you a way to consider this idea of just enough support.

COACH YOURSELF CONFIDENT #36

 REFLECTION: The challenge continuum

Step 1

If you have a manager, think about your current experience of them. In what ways are they actively challenging you, encouraging you to take on new things? In what ways are they helping to keep you safe, avoiding situations for which you're not yet ready?

If you work for yourself, think about the extent to which you push yourself to do new things or to step forward before you feel 100% prepared. And think about how you keep yourself safe from stretching too far.

Step 2

How does this combination of challenge and safety leave you feeling – where would you place yourself on the continuum below?

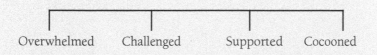

Overwhelmed   Challenged   Supported   Cocooned

Step 3

What comes up for you as you look at where you've placed yourself on the continuum? Is there a conversation that you'd like to have with your manager? Is there a reset to do on the extent to which you challenge yourself?

Keeping up with yourself

'One of the things I'm conscious of, having stayed with the organization for over 25 years, is that there's still a bit of me that feels like a graduate trainee who's trying to prove herself.' This was what Rebecca Snow said to me as she reflected on the nuanced ups and downs of her confidence. Rebecca is now Global Vice President for HR for Mars Snacking, an organization of 30,000 people. She has built a very successful career in the organization, fulfilling a range of roles in different functions and geographies before progressing to the most senior level of the business. And yet, in a sense she hasn't fully kept up with herself, part of her identity remains the 22-year-old graduate trainee who joined the business back in 1995. Rebecca's awareness serves her well – knowing that the young graduate trainee with a fair degree of self-doubt and a need to prove remains within her means that she can spot the times when old patterns resurface and she can reset her confidence.

This thread about keeping up with oneself came up in my conversation with Ben Lamont, another successful HR leader, currently a Senior HR Director at Kellanova. Ben told me: 'I still see myself as a sales rep in 2000 selling crisps in Scotland. And then suddenly I go "how am I in conversation with this person or this person?" I still think of myself as less experienced, less mature and less developed, and then I find myself in a situation and go "how did that happen?" It's very good from a grounding point of view, but I think I have to watch that it doesn't have an adverse effect on my impact.' Ben sees the upside to this throwback to his more junior self – there's a likeable humility that comes with it – and he rightly sees a watch out too.

COACH YOURSELF CONFIDENT #37

 REFLECTION: Keeping up with yourself

Did Rebecca or Ben's story resonate with you? Do you sometimes wonder how you got to the place that you find yourself today?

This is a short activity that might help to shed light on a 'I'm still the trainee' story if such a story is sitting quietly somewhere in your mind. Perhaps it will help you to smile about it in the way that both Rebecca and Ben did.

First write down the job titles or a one-line description of the roles that you've had since the start of your career.

Now take a few minutes to read through your list. Your brain might want to scan through quickly because this information is already known but try to slow yourself down and really read what you've noted. Your aim is to fully acknowledge your progress, whether that be vertical or horizontal.

Permission to be you

'No need to hurry. No need to sparkle. No need to be anybody but oneself.' These wonderful words come from Virginia Woolf's essay *A Room of One's Own*. They point to one of the most significant things that you can do to grow your confidence from the inside: give yourself full permission to be who you are. This means being clear about your values, being clear about the impact that you want to have on those around you, being clear on the impact you want to have in your organization or on wider society. This clarity comes from the inside – it's your own version of 'success', not shaped by what we perceive to be the expectations of others. In an organization setting, it's about *choosing* how you will do your role, setting aside any sense of obligation or 'should'. In doing this – in creating your own version of what good looks like – you set out to do the role in a way that's unique to you, and in so doing, you set yourself up for success.

My final interview in the research phase for this book was with the headteacher of an independent girls school who I will call Michelle. Michelle is in her first headteacher post, and reflected on how challenging she found the transition from Deputy Head to Head. 'These last four years have tested my confidence in myself more than anything.' Michelle described the feeling of being 'completely de-skilled' as she moved from a school that she knew inside out into a completely unknown setting. 'I didn't even know where the photocopier was, or where to get a cup of tea.' Stepping up to the headship meant becoming the ultimate decision maker, and Michelle felt this responsibility keenly, aware that she was making judgements that could affect the future of a pupil or the future of the school. The headship also brought a greater degree of visibility – being in the limelight in a way that she hadn't previously experienced. Add to this the experience of leading the school through the Covid-19 pandemic and it's not difficult to see why Michelle's confidence was tested.

Four years after her arrival at the school, Michelle is significantly more confident in her role. The evidence of what she has been able to do during these first years in the top leadership position contributes to this increased feeling of assurance. I imagine that there's a dose of *if I can get through a global pandemic, I can get through anything* in there too. Perhaps the bigger factor in her increased confidence has been the way that Michelle has found *her way* of being a headteacher. It's inevitable that those around her – teachers, students, parents, governors – all have their own mental model of a good headteacher, they have their own set of expectations. Michelle is attuned to this array of expectations – she has to be – but she is not constrained or overly-influenced by them. 'When I first took on the role, it's as though I put on a cloak of headship which didn't really fit me – it was a cloak that represented the way I thought a headteacher should be.

But as I grew into the role, I discarded the cloak, seeing that it wasn't needed. I now have the confidence to be the kind of Head that I am. I'm not going to be the remote, austere figure. I'm not like that. I'm like this.'

I think it's a wonderful final story for this book, bringing to life as it does the liberating power of giving yourself permission to be you. And it's the platform for the final *Coach Yourself Confident* exercise, which is a framework for you to reflect on the extent to which you give yourself permission to be you.

COACH YOURSELF CONFIDENT #38

 REFLECTION: Permission to be you

I offer you three lines of enquiry as you consider the extent to which you give yourself permission to be you. I invite you to ponder on these questions and note down your thoughts.

Enquiry 1

To what extent do you give yourself 'permission to be you' in the way that you do your current role?

Are you wearing the 'cloak' of expectation in the way that Michelle initially did, or have you set out your own path?

Enquiry 2

Go back to the values that you identified in Coach
Yourself Confident #14 in Chapter 3. How do your
values show up in the way that you work? How
evident are they to the people around you?

Enquiry 3

Would those who know you in a non-work setting
recognize you in work? Would there be anything
about the 'work you' that surprises them?

If so, what do you make of that? What might it
suggest about your current permission to be you?

To sum up...

- Homegrown confidence is a robust belief in yourself that is grown from within.

- Praise from others, new qualifications, the status that comes with a new job title or grade – all of these things can make a difference to how you feel about yourself, triggering pride and swelling confidence.

- Unless you use these external confidence boosts as a catalyst to update your self-image and reappraise your sense of your own capability, the lift in confidence will be fleeting.

- Caring too much about what people think of us leaves us vulnerable; we can only have self-trust if others trust in our skills and abilities. It builds our confidence when others offer praise, but confidence can crash when they criticize.

- With support, it's easier to take action, easier to navigate setbacks, easier to pull out the learnings when things don't go to plan, easier to celebrate successes when they do. We can grow our confidence in community with others, internalizing the messages from our cheerleaders and making the most of *just enough* support to both reassure and stretch us.

- One of the most significant things that you can do to grow your confidence from the inside is to give yourself permission to be who you are. To be uniquely you.

A few final words of encouragement

Confidence is the trust in yourself that whatever the situation, whatever life throws at you, you will be OK. You will have the resources you need; you will find a way through. It's fuel for life. Our aim has been to grow your confidence so that it aligns with your capability, enabling you to see yourself in the way that your supporters see you and to acknowledge and own the many strengths that you bring. This is humble confidence, underpinned by the understanding that you are good enough *and* you can be better. It's the kind of confidence that enables growth and avoids complacency. In unlocking the realistic view of your capability that humble confidence brings, you can right-size your self-doubt and you can ditch the self-doubt tax.

I hope that your confidence fuel gauge has registered an uplift as you've read the last seven chapters, completed the reflection activities and tried out the practices. You've reached the final few pages of the book, but of course this is not the end of your efforts to grow your confidence. Developing belief in yourself is not the sort of work that has an end; there isn't really a point at which you can tick it off your to-do list and proclaim that you're done. Confidence built – tick! (I recognize that this truth is tricky for those of us who are addicted to achievement or to perfection.)

What you will experience as you move forward is the gradual lessening of the self-doubt tax that you're paying, alongside the complementary growth of your trust in yourself. These changes might not feel obvious on a day-to-day basis (a bit like the way in which we don't notice children getting taller in real time), but they accumulate in a way that ultimately makes a real difference.

Keep trying out the *Coach Yourself Confident* practices and remember to take a step back every so often to notice and appreciate the progress that you're making. My final invitation to you as we reach the end of the book is to look back now at the confidence aspiration that you set out when you began reading the book (this was Coach Yourself Confident #2 which was a part of Chapter 1) and to think about the ways in which you have already made small steps. All of these small steps matter because over time they add up to significant growth.

Keep going. I'm delighted that you've come this far and I know that you can continue to grow your confidence. I have every faith in you.

Acknowledgements

As I set out to write the book, I imagined that authorship would be quite a solitary activity. But I was wrong. Whilst there have been many hours during which I've been alone with the process of marshalling my thinking into a coherent shape, perhaps the most enjoyable part of the process has been creating this book in community with others. There are many people to thank.

Stories are at the heart of the book and I am incredibly grateful to my interviewees for agreeing to talk to me and for sharing your experiences so generously. Thank you to Si Bradley, Mark Chamberlen, Sarah Dickens, Chris Fawkes, Ben Lamont, Miranda Mapleton, Fiona Miles, Uma Rajah, Kate Richardson-Walsh OBE, Matt Ridsdale, Lindsay Rowe and Rebecca Snow.

Thank you to my fellow coaches and practitioners for listening to my early ideas and adding your wisdom into the blend of thinking that became the book. Simon Cavicchia, Steve Chapman, Julian Powe and Gail Sulkes. And an additional thank you to Simon for supporting me to work through the ups and downs in my own confidence as I wrote a book about confidence. Our supervision relationship continues to be invaluable to me.

My team of early readers – you have all left your mark on the book, helping to improve it enormously in the process. Thank you Lucy Ball, Dan Bethell, Lynne Fantham, Carrie Goucher (special thanks for your 11–7 rule!), Becky Hall, Miranda

Mapleton, Richard Rosenberg and Andy Smith. A huge thank you also to my two development editors: Catherine Flack and Kate Llewellyn – your blend of encouragement and constructive criticism was much appreciated. And Lesley Cooper, copy editor extraordinaire, I'm in awe of your diligence and attention to detail. You polished the copy beautifully, thank you.

Big virtual high five to everyone who got involved via LinkedIn, particularly to Andy Brett, Kim Stokes and Evelyn Van Orden for allowing me to use your comments in the book. And thank you Claire Robertson – did you spot the beautiful turn of phrase that I borrowed from your LinkedIn comment?

Thanks also to Stef Reid for your encouragement through the process and for allowing me to include some extracts from your appearance on the High Performance podcast. And thank you to Phil Taylor, the warm and inclusive leader who pulled me into the circle at that leadership programme 17 years ago – both for what you did at the time and for so readily agreeing to the story being included in the book.

Coach Yourself Confident began its life during the ten-day book proposal challenge in January 2023 run by the wonderful Alison Jones. I am grateful for the support and solidarity from fellow challengers during those ten days and the months that followed as we created our books alongside one another. Thanks to all of you, in particular Rebecca Arora, Oliver Banks and Philippa White. I'm looking forward to reading your books.

I've been cheered on by so many people since I announced my intention to write. A huge thank you to my family, the fabulous PepsiCo alumni, my Primrose Hill supervision group and my book club. And to all my friends for your enthusiasm, curiosity and many messages of encouragement.

I've left two of the biggest thank yous to the end. Caroline Chapple, working with you on the illustrations was joyous. You pushed me to clarify my thinking and hone the key concepts, and your contribution goes beyond the wonderful illustrations you created. Our conversations helped me tighten up my thinking and as a result, my writing. Thank you.

And finally, Alison Jones and the whole Practical Inspiration Publishing team. You've been there every step of the way providing the support, encouragement and advice that I needed. The book proposal challenge set me on the path to creating a book that I'm proud of. You have my lasting gratitude for enabling me to convert an idea in my head into a book on my bookshelf.

About the author

Julie Smith is a sought-after executive coach whose experience spans three decades. A 15+ year corporate career with Mars and PepsiCo gave Julie first-hand experience of what it takes to succeed in a demanding, fast-paced organization.

In 2010, Julie founded Talent Sprout, a highly respected leadership consultancy. The business name reflects Julie's passion for helping people and organizations to grow. In her coaching and consulting work, Julie works with leaders to grow their impact, supports teams to grow their effectiveness and supports organizations to grow their profits by fully harnessing the talent and energy of their people.

Julie has coached hundreds of executives and leadership teams both in the UK and internationally, working with well-known organizations across sectors ranging from packaged consumer goods to technology, insurance to luxury goods and banking to hospitality.

Described by her clients as insightful, collaborative and 'one of the best in her field', Julie has designed and delivered development programmes that participants find 'life changing'.

If you're interested in talking to Julie about coaching, consulting or speaking opportunities, visit www.talentsprout. co.uk.

Bibliography

Brown, Brené. *Atlas of the Heart: Mapping Meaningful Connection and the Language of Human Experience.* Vermilion. 2021.

Brown, Brené. *Dare to Lead: Brave Work. Tough Conversations. Whole Hearts.* Vermilion. 2018.

Chamorro-Premuzic, Tomas. *Confidence: The Surprising Truth About How Much You Need and How to Get It.* Profile Books. 2013.

Cuddy, Amy. Inside the Debate about Power Posing: A Q&A with Amy Cuddy. Ideas.Ted.Com. 2017. https://ideas.ted.com/inside-the-debate-about-power-posing-a-q-a-with-amy-cuddy

Day, Elizabeth. *Failosophy: A Handbook for When Things Go Wrong.* 4th Estate. 2020.

Day, Elizabeth. *How to Fail: Everything I've Ever Learned From Things Going Wrong.* 4th Estate. 2019.

De Botton, Alain and The School of Life. *The School of Life: An Emotional Education.* Hamish Hamilton. 2019.

Doyle, Glennon. *Untamed: Stop Pleasing, Start Living.* Vermilion. 2020.

Dweck, Dr Carol. *Mindset: Changing The Way You Think to Fulfil Your Potential.* Robinson. 2012.

Flintoff, John-Paul. *A Modest Book About How to Make an Adequate Speech*. Short Books. 2021.

Gallwey, Timothy W. *The Inner Game of Tennis*. Pan Books. 1986.

Gallwey, Timothy W. *The Inner Game of Work*. Villard Books. 1998.

Gannon, Emma. *Sabotage: How to Silence Your Inner Critic and Get Out of Your Own Way*. Hodder & Stoughton. 2020.

Groskop, Viv. *Happy High Status: How to Be Effortlessly Confident*. Transworld Digital. 2023.

Hall, Becky. *The Art of Enough: 7 Ways to Build a Balanced Life and a Flourishing World*. Practical Inspiration Publishing. 2021.

Hardy, Dr Benjamin and Sullivan, Dan. *The Gap and the Gain*. Hay House UK. 2021.

Harris, Dr Russ. *The Confidence Gap: From Fear to Freedom*. Robinson. 2011.

Hibberd, Dr Jessamy. *The Imposter Cure: How to Stop Feeling like a Fraud and Escape the Mind-Trap of Imposter Syndrome*. Aster. 2019.

Hollis, James. *Creating a Life: Finding Your Individual Path*. Inner City Books. 2001.

Höpfner, Jessica and Keith, Nina. 'Goal missed, self hit: Goal-setting, goal-failure, and their affective, motivational, and behavioral consequences'. *Frontiers in Psychology*. 12:704790. 2021. doi:10.3389/fpsyg.2021.704790

Humphries, Jake and Hughes, Damien. The High Performance Podcast. www.thehighperformancepodcast.com

Jeffers, Susan. *Feal the Fear and Do It Anyway*. Arrow Books. 1991.

Jerrim, John, Parker, Phil and Shure, Nikki. 'Bullshitters: Who are they and what do we know about their lives?' *Institute of Labor Economics*. No. 12282. 2019. www.iza.org/publications/dp/12282/bullshitters-who-are-they-and-what-do-we-know-about-their-lives

Jones, Jessica. *Own It: How to Build Confidence, Completely Love Yourself, and Embrace Your Body*. Welbeck Balance. 2022.

Kay, Katty and Shipman, Claire. *The Confidence Code: The Science and Art of Self-Assurance – What Women Should Know*. Harper Collins eBooks. 2014.

King, Zella and Scott, Amanda. *Who Is in Your Personal Boardroom? How to Choose People, Assign Roles and Have Conversations with Purpose*. CreateSpace Independent Publishing Platform. 2014.

Kishimi, Ichiro and Koga, Fumitake. *The Courage to be Disliked: How to Free Yourself, Change Your Life and Achieve Real Happiness*. Allen & Unwin. 2018.

Kross, Ethan. *Chatter: The Voice in Our Head and How to Harness It*. Vermilion. 2021.

Lamott, Anne. *Bird by Bird: Instructions on Writing and Life*. Canongate Canons. 2020.

Lemola, Sakari, Räikkönen, Katri, Gomez, Veronica and Allemand, Mathias. 'Optimism and self-esteem are related to sleep. Results from a large community-based sample'. *International Journal of Behavioural Medicine*. 20, 567–571. 2013. https://doi.org/10.1007/s12529-012-9272-z

Lewis, Sarah. *The Rise: Creativity, the Gift of Failure, and the Search for Mastery*. William Collins. 2015.

Mathur, Anna. *Know Your Worth: How To Build Your Self-Esteem, Grow in Confidence and Worry Less About What People Think*. Piatkus. 2021.

Merzenich, Dr Michael. *Soft-Wired: How the New Science of Brain Plasticity Can Change Your Life*. Parnassus Publishing. 2013.

Nadal, Rafael and Carlin, John. *Rafa: My Story*. Hachette Books. 2013.

Neff, Dr Kristin. Self-Compassion. https://self-compassion. org

Nugent, Richard. *The 50 Secrets of Self-Confidence: The Confidence To Do Whatever You Want To Do*. William Collins. 2015.

Pépin, Charles. *Self-Confidence: A Philosophy*. William Collins. 2020.

Pink, Daniel H. *To Sell is Human: The Surprising Truth About Persuading, Convincing and Influencing Others*. Canongate Books. 2014.

Price, Paul C. and Stone, Eric R. 'Intuitive evaluation of likelihood judgment producers: Evidence for a confidence heuristic'. *Journal of Behavioral Decision Making*, 17(1), 39–58. 2004. https://doi.org/10.1002/bdm.460

Pulford, Briony D., Colman, Andrew M., Buabang, Eike K. and Krockow, Eva M. 'The persuasive power of knowledge: Testing the confidence heuristic'. *Journal of Experimental Psychology: General,* 147(10), 1431–1444. https://psycnet.apa.org/fulltext/2018-41338-001.html

Robertson, Ian. *How Confidence Works: The New Science of Self-Belief.* Transworld Digital. Kindle Edition. 2021.

Schafler, Katherine Morgan. *The Perfectionist's Guide to Losing Control.* Orion Spring. 2023.

Seligman, Martin E.P. *Learned Optimism: How to Change Your Mind and Your Life.* Vintage Books. 2006.

Smith, James. *How to Be Confident.* HarperCollins Publishers. 2022.

Smith, Dr Julie. *Why Has Nobody Told Me This Before?* Penguin Books. 2022.

Stewart, Ian and Joines, Vann. *TA Today: A New Introduction to Transactional Analysis.* Lifespace Publishing. 1987.

Tenney, Elizabeth R. and Spellman, Barbara A. 'Complex social consequences of self-knowledge'. *Social Psychological & Personality Science,* 2(4), 343–350. 2010. https://journals.sagepub.com/doi/10.1177/1948550610390965

The School of Life. *On Confidence.* The School of Life Press. 2017.

The School of Life. *On Failure.* The School of Life Press. 2022.

Tupper, Helen and Ellis, Sarah. *The Squiggly Career: Ditch the Ladder, Discover Opportunity, Design Your Career.* Penguin Books. 2020.

Index

A quick word from Practical Inspiration Publishing...

We hope you found this book both practical and inspiring – that's what we aim for with every book we publish.

We publish titles on topics ranging from leadership, entrepreneurship, HR and marketing to self-development and wellbeing.

Find details of all our books at: www.practicalinspiration.com

 Did you know...

We can offer discounts on bulk sales of all our titles – ideal if you want to use them for training purposes, corporate giveaways or simply because you feel these ideas deserve to be shared with your network.

We can even produce bespoke versions of our books, for example with your organization's logo and/or a tailored foreword.

To discuss further, contact us on info@practicalinspiration.com.

 Got an idea for a business book?

We may be able to help. Find out more about publishing in partnership with us at: bit.ly/PIpublishing.

Follow us on social media...

 @PIPTalking

 @pip_talking

 @practicalinspiration

 @piptalking

 Practical Inspiration Publishing

Printed in the USA
CPSIA information can be obtained
at www.ICGtesting.com
JSHW042026130524
63053JS00018B/480